BLUE-COLLAR BOSS

BLUE-COLLAR BOSS

Hard Work Builds It.
Leadership Keeps It.

MARK STONER

Blue-Collar Boss:
Hard Work Builds It. Leadership Keeps It.

Published by Blue Collar Enterprises

First Edition

ISBN: 978-1-7331818-2-2 (Paperback)

ISBN: 978-1-7331818-5-3 (Hardcover)

ISBN: 978-1-7331818-4-6 (eBook)

ISBN: 978-1-7331818-3-9 (Audiobook)

Cover design and interior formatting by Becky's Graphic Design®, LLC
www.BeckysGraphicDesign.com

Images are licensed from Adobe Stock and used with permission.
Author photo by Judith Hill Photography.

For my family.

For Terry, my wife, who has walked beside me
through every high and low, never wavering in her
belief in me, even when I questioned myself.

For my son Saxon, who has always been thinking ahead, spotting
gaps I couldn't yet see, and pushing me to build what was missing.

For my daughter Evane, a tireless entrepreneur in her own right,
growing into an incredible boss with courage, discipline, and heart.

All of my current and past employees that have
stood with me while I learned leadership!

And for the men and women who show up every day in blue-
collar work, carrying responsibility most people never see.

This book is for you.

Contents

BECOME THE KIND OF
BOSS THAT
BUSINESS REQUIRES
TO SURVIVE —
AND THRIVE — AT SCALE.
— MARK STONER

From Blue-Collar Gold to Blue-Collar Boss

When I wrote *Blue-Collar Gold*, I was still in the middle of the climb.

That book came from building something from nothing — learning through scraped knuckles, long nights, and mistakes you can't Google your way out of. It was written for people in the trenches, trying to figure out how to turn hard work into something sustainable.

I didn't know if anyone would read it.

Since then, *Blue-Collar Gold* has sold more than **50,000 copies worldwide.** It's been shared in shops, passed between friends, highlighted, dog-eared, and used as a kind of field manual by owners in blue-collar businesses around the world.

That response humbled me.

But more importantly, it showed me something.

As businesses grow, the challenges change.

The questions I started getting weren't about starting anymore. They were about leading. About culture. About accountability. About systems. About people. About what to do when effort alone stops scaling.

That's what Blue-Collar Boss is about.

This book is not a rewrite of *Blue-Collar Gold*. It's not a sequel that assumes you know the backstory. And it's not a theory book built from hindsight.

It's the next phase.

If *Blue-Collar Gold* was about building the business, *Blue-Collar Boss* is about becoming the kind of boss that business requires to survive — and thrive — at scale.

You do not need to have read the first book to get value from this one. But if you have, you'll recognize the throughline: honesty, responsibility, and a refusal to sugarcoat what leadership actually demands.

Different season.

Different pressure.

Same commitment to telling the truth.

Now let's get to work.

Mark Stoner
February 2026

Introduction

This book exists because of people who lived these lessons with me.

Thank you to the employees and former employees of Ashbusters and my other companies. You helped shape these systems, these decisions, and these hard-earned lessons. Many of the ideas in this book were forged in real moments with real consequences alongside you.

Thank you to the mentors and friends who challenged my thinking and pushed me forward when growth required discomfort.

And thank you to every blue-collar business owner who has shared their stories with me over the years. Your struggles, questions, and honesty reinforced why this work matters.

I Want to Be in Your Seat

He was quitting that day.

A young, talented, hard-working technician sat across from my desk and told me he was done.

He wasn't angry. He wasn't dramatic. He was calm, confident, and certain. That almost made it worse.

I asked him why. Not defensively. Genuinely. I didn't see it coming, and when you've been in business long enough, the surprises are usually what hurt the most.

He leaned back in the chair, pointed at my desk, and said,

"I want to be in that seat."

I knew exactly what he meant. And I also knew exactly what he couldn't see.

From where he stood, that seat looked powerful. Free. Secure. It looked like control. It looked like success. It looked like arrival.

So I told him something that surprised both of us.

"You wouldn't want that seat at your age."

He looked confused, almost offended. I explained.

That seat looks pretty good at fifty-two.

It looks brutal at twenty-two.

From where he stood, he could see the results. He couldn't see the pressure. He couldn't see the responsibility. He couldn't see the nights spent staring at the ceiling, the mornings where calm was the only thing keeping the business from unraveling, or the decisions where there was no right answer—only consequences.

I told him that leadership isn't something you step into. It's something you acclimate to.

I used the Mount Everest analogy, because it's the only one that really fits.

If you were dropped on the top of Everest tomorrow, you'd be dead within minutes. Not because you're weak, but because your body hasn't adapted to the pressure. Real climbers don't start at the summit. They train for months, sometimes years. They climb to Base Camp One, then back down. Then Base Camp Two. Sometimes they retreat. Sometimes they wait.

Slowly, deliberately, their bodies adapt.

Only then do they make a summit push—and even then, they can only stay briefly before the mountain forces them back down.

Leadership works the same way.

Everyone wants the seat.

Very few understand the climb.

This book is about that climb.

Not the highlight reel.

Not the myths.

The real work of becoming the kind of boss who can carry pressure without breaking people—and build something that lasts beyond themselves.

CHAPTER 2

Boss Isn't a Dirty Word

Somewhere along the way, the word *boss* became a punchline.

We were told bosses were outdated. That leadership meant soft language, consensus, and endless collaboration. That authority should apologize for existing. That being firm meant being toxic.

That thinking has done real damage in blue-collar businesses.

Because blue-collar work does not need less authority.

It needs better authority.

I'm not interested in being a tyrant. I'm not interested in being a buddy. And I'm not interested in pretending structure isn't necessary in environments that are physical, dangerous, fast-moving, and unforgiving.

Early in my career, I tried to lead by being agreeable. I listened well. I cared deeply. I assumed good intent. I thought if people understood *why*, they would naturally do the right thing.

What I didn't understand yet was this: **clarity doesn't come from being liked.**

It comes from being decisive.

I watched confusion creep in slowly.

Standards blurred.

Expectations softened.

People started asking the same questions over and over—not because they didn't understand, but because the answers kept changing depending on the day, the person, or the situation.

My calm, which I believed was maturity, was being interpreted as uncertainty.

And uncertainty creates anxiety faster than any bad decision ever will.

A good boss brings direction.

A great boss brings calm *and* clarity.

The turning point for me was realizing that my team didn't need me to be softer. They needed me to be clearer. They needed someone willing to say, "This is the standard," and then defend it—especially when it was uncomfortable.

Being a boss doesn't mean domination.

It means responsibility.

When people know where the line is, they relax. When they know it won't move based on mood or pressure, trust grows. Structure doesn't suffocate good people—it frees them.

The problem was never the word *boss*.

The problem was weak bossing.

THE LEADERSHIP PRINCIPLES

- Leadership looks easier from the outside than it feels on the inside.
- Desire does not equal readiness.
- Pressure reveals gaps you can't see from below.
- Promoting too early hurts good people.
- The boss's job is to protect people from weight they're not ready to carry.

THE VIDEO YOU SHOULD RECORD

Record a video titled: **"What That Seat Really Costs"**

Explain:

- What leadership actually demands emotionally.
- What pressure you didn't expect.
- Why you don't rush people into responsibility.
- What "earning the seat" really means.

This video reframes ambition into maturity.

THREE THINGS TO DO THIS WEEK

1. Identify one person who *wants* more responsibility but may not be ready.
2. Identify one person who *is* ready but hasn't raised their hand.
3. Write down the real pressures of your role — not the perks.

CLARITY DOESN'T COME FROM BEING LIKED. IT COMES FROM BEING DECISIVE.

— MARK STONER

CHAPTER 3

Fear Always Comes First

Looking back, it's easy to connect the dots and pretend confidence led the way.

It didn't.

Fear did.

Fear has been present at every meaningful turning point in my career. Not fear that stopped me completely — but fear that slowed decisions, softened commitments, and convinced me to wait just a little longer than I should have.

Early on, I thought fear was a sign I was doing something wrong.

Now I understand it was usually a sign I was about to grow.

The First Time the Numbers Scared Me

There was a point early in Ashbusters where things were finally starting to work.

We weren't rich.

We weren't comfortable.

But we were stable enough that I could breathe between paydays.

That stability felt fragile.

Then I was faced with a decision that scared the hell out of me: hiring a Chief Operations Officer that required a six-figure **overhead** position.

Up to that point, I'd had technicians making six figures — and I loved that. They were production-based. They earned it. It made sense to me. Big work, big checks.

This was different.

This person didn't "produce" revenue the way a technician did. Their value would be indirect. Systems. People. Operations.

And I remember thinking, *Who am I to pay someone that much when I'm just now making a decent living myself?*

That fear wasn't logical.

It was emotional.

And it sat heavy.

The Lie I Told Myself

I told myself I was being responsible.

"I just need to be sure."

"Let's wait one more quarter."

"I'll handle it myself for now."

What I was really saying was: *I don't trust this enough yet.*

Not the person.

Not the role.

Not myself.

The truth is, waiting felt safer than committing.

And it cost me.

Fear Always Charges Interest

Here's what no one tells you about fear: It doesn't just pause progress — it **charges interest**.

While I waited:

- problems stacked up
- decisions slowed
- people waited on me
- energy drained

I was busy, but not effective.

I was involved everywhere, but leading nowhere.

That's when something finally clicked for me:

If the right hire doesn't make you money, you hired the wrong person — not the wrong role.

When I Finally Stepped Through It

When I finally made that hire, the result wasn't immediate relief.

It was discomfort.

Suddenly, I wasn't the smartest person in the room anymore.

Suddenly, my instincts were being challenged.

Suddenly, systems were being questioned.

That was unsettling.

But within months, something else happened.

Decisions got better.

Problems surfaced sooner.

I got time back.

And the most surprising part?

The business didn't just grow — **it stabilized.**

The hire didn't cost me money. They freed it.

They didn't take control. They gave me leverage.

Growth Always Asks for Trust First

Every major growth move since then has followed the same pattern.

Fear first.

Rationalization second.

Growth only after commitment.

New locations. Price increases. Systems changes. Letting go of people I liked.

Every time, fear showed up early and loud.

And every time I tried to outthink it instead of walk through it, growth stalled.

The Mistake I Made More Than Once

I wish I could say I learned this lesson once and never repeated it.

I didn't.

I delayed hard conversations because I didn't want conflict.
I avoided raising prices because I didn't want pushback.
I held onto roles too long because I didn't want to feel replaceable.

Each time, fear disguised itself as caution.

I have a program called Blue-Collar University where I work with other business owners, office staff and techs to make them better. They all have very similar problems and many of the solutions are to just execute, decide and move. . . .now.

Each time, the cost showed up later — bigger than if I'd acted sooner.

What I Understand Now

Fear is not the enemy.

Misinterpreting fear is.

Fear doesn't mean stop. Fear usually means *pay attention*.

It's the toll booth before the bridge.

And every meaningful bridge charges something.

Money.

Ego.

Comfort.

Control.

You don't get to cross without paying.

Why This Matters to You

If you're reading this and facing a decision that feels heavy — a hire, a system change, a price increase, a confrontation — I want you to hear this clearly:

The fear you feel is not proof you're unqualified.

It's proof the decision matters.

Confidence doesn't come first. Commitment does.

Confidence shows up later.

The Seat Feels Different On the Other Side

Once you walk through fear a few times, something changes.

You stop expecting certainty. You stop waiting for perfect timing. You start trusting process over comfort.

The boss's seat doesn't get lighter — but you get stronger.

And eventually, fear stops being a warning sign.

It becomes a signal.

The Lesson That Stuck

The biggest shift for me was realizing this:

Make decisions very quickly, You will never have all of the information. Things change **after** the decision is made anyway so be expecting the shift after the action that you took. Working with business owners that can't decide quickly is so frustrating to me. Even when I go to lunches or dinners with people great leaders and decisive people make their decisions quickly.

That doesn't mean reckless. It means intentional.

Growth doesn't reward hesitation. It rewards action — even imperfect action.

Looking Back Honestly

If I could talk to myself at that stage — white-knuckling decisions and trying to protect every dollar — I'd tell him this:

You don't need certainty to move forward.

You need some clarity and mostly courage.

Things can go wrong and you will make it.

The fear won't disappear. But it will stop controlling you once you stop obeying it.

When Safety Becomes the Risk

There have been many moments in my business career where I've had to walk straight into the fire.

They're never comfortable.

They're never clean.

And they're never obvious when you're standing in them.

But this was the first one that really showed me what leadership was going to cost.

Early on, I was running the business out of my house.

At the time, it made sense. It was cheap. It was familiar. It felt safe.

My house worked — until it didn't.

Trucks started delivering materials to my driveway.

Employees parked at my house and ran into my wife's car. Not once. Multiple times.

People showed up on weekends. Late nights. Early mornings.

I couldn't escape it.

My home wasn't a home anymore. It was a job site.

To make it worse, I was using storage units. One turned into two. Then bigger ones. Then more. I told myself it was temporary.

That's a lie fear tells you to buy time.

The Conversation I Didn't Want to Hear

One day, my landlord asked me a question that caught me completely off guard.

"When are you going to get serious about your business?"

I remember feeling defensive.

"What do you mean?"

He didn't hesitate.

"You're running a business out of storage units and your bedroom. It's time to grow up and have a real office."

Then he said the part that scared me.

"I have space that would be perfect for you."

I asked how much.

"Six hundred dollars a month. Twelve hundred square feet."

Today that sounds laughable. Back then, it felt enormous.

I wasn't making much money. Margins were thin. Everything felt fragile.

But he was right — and I knew it.

The First Step Into the Fire

Signing that lease felt reckless.

But the moment we moved in, something changed.

Not because we suddenly knew what we were doing — but because the environment demanded more of me.

We grew fast.

We grew messy.

We made mistakes.

But I had crossed a line I couldn't uncross. I was no longer pretending to run a business. I was responsible for one.

Not long after, a 5,000-square-foot building opened up across the street.

In my mind, it was massive.

Way too big.

Way too expensive.

We moved anyway.

And almost immediately, the 2008–2009 housing crisis hit.

I lost everything.

I couldn't pay rent. I couldn't pay utilities. I couldn't pay payroll. I couldn't pay myself.

There were days I sat in that building completely alone.

Terrified. Broke. And strangely, a little free.

Because once everything falls apart, the fear changes.

You stop trying to protect what's already gone.

The Lesson That Stayed With Me

That building didn't ruin me. Staying small would have.

Since then, we've moved many times. Each time into something bigger. Each time it's been scary. Each time it cost more than I expected. Each time it didn't go the way I thought it would.

That's growth.

Every real barrier in business looks like this.

It's not a wall — it's a fire.

You don't get certainty first. You don't get confidence first. You get a choice.

Stay safe and slowly cap your future —or take a deep breath and step forward.

That's leadership.

THE LEADERSHIP PRINCIPLES

1. Fear often signals the edge of growth.
2. Overhead hires feel dangerous until they unlock scale.
3. Effort stops scaling before leaders do.
4. The right hire creates time, not expense.
5. Control must decrease for growth to increase.

THE VIDEO YOU SHOULD RECORD

Title it: **"The Scariest Hire I Ever Made"**

Explain:

- What made it scary?
- What almost stopped you?
- What changed afterward?
- What you would do sooner next time?

This gives permission for courageous decisions.

THREE THINGS TO DO THIS WEEK

1. List decisions you've delayed because they feel expensive or risky.
2. Identify where you are the bottleneck.
3. Ask: "What hire would give me the most leverage?"

CHAPTER 4

When Effort Stopped Working

For a long time, effort was my advantage.

If something broke, I worked harder.

If we fell behind, I stayed later.

If someone quit, I filled the gap.

And it worked.

That's the dangerous part — **it works long enough to trap you.**

In the early years, effort feels like leadership. Sweat feels like commitment. Exhaustion feels like proof you care.

But somewhere along the way, effort quietly stops producing results — and starts hiding problems instead.

The Season When Nothing Felt Finished

There was a stretch where the company was growing, but nothing felt under control.

Revenue was up.

Headcount was up.

Locations were expanding.

And yet every day felt reactive.

I'd fix one issue, only to uncover three more.

I'd make a decision in the morning and reverse it by afternoon.

I'd leave the office feeling productive — and come back to chaos.

The hardest part wasn't the workload.

It was the feeling that **no matter how hard I worked, the business still needed me everywhere.**

That should have been a warning sign.

I treated it like a badge of honor.

The Trap of Being the Fixer

Looking back, I can see how much of my identity was wrapped up in being the solution.

If I wasn't needed, what did that say about my value?

So I stayed involved.

I stayed central.

I stayed indispensable.

And without realizing it, I trained the company to depend on me.

People waited instead of deciding.

Problems escalated instead of resolving.

Systems stayed informal because I could "just handle it."

That's when effort quietly became the bottleneck.

The Moment It Finally Hit Me

There wasn't a single dramatic event.

It was more like death by a thousand interruptions.

Phone calls that couldn't wait.

Questions that should've been answered without me.

Decisions that required my input because no one else felt authorized.

One day I realized something unsettling:

If I stepped away for more than a few days, things slowed down.

Not because people were lazy — but because **nothing had been built to function without me.**

That realization didn't feel empowering.

It felt heavy.

Here's what I understand now that I didn't then:

Effort is not leadership.

Effort is survival.

It's necessary early.

It's noble early.

It's unavoidable early.

But it has an expiration date.

If effort is still your primary strategy at scale, you're not leading — you're compensating.

When You Don't Step In, the World Will

There was a situation early in my career that still sticks with me — mostly because of how badly it could have ended.

Two younger guys on my team were apprentices. Both had big personalities. Both were competitive. And they didn't like each other.

At first, it was just chirping.

Trash talk.

Needling.

Ego stuff.

I didn't really know how bad it had gotten. I knew there was tension, but I didn't realize how far it had escalated.

And that was my first mistake.

One day, instead of bringing it to me, they decided to settle it themselves.

They picked a park.

Now, they were smart enough not to fight at the shop. They knew better than that. But what I didn't know was that several other employees knew about the fight and went to watch.

This was probably around 2000 or 2004 — a long time ago. I've learned a lot since then. This does not happen in today's Ashbusters.

But back then, it happened.

The Fight That Wasn't Ours to Have

They went to a city park and started fighting.

And it wasn't even close. One kid was clearly beating the other one.

What they didn't know — what *none* of them knew — was that this park wasn't neutral ground.

It belonged to a gang.

A Mexican gang.

And they were not happy that a bunch of guys showed up in their park to fight like idiots.

Suddenly, the whole situation flipped.

If you've ever seen a movie where two enemies are fighting each other and then a bigger threat shows up — and all of a sudden, the people who hated each other are on the same side — that's exactly what happened.

In an instant, my employees stopped being enemies.

They were surrounded.

When Things Go Very, Very Wrong

The gang came out with bats and crowbars.

They started smashing cars.

Breaking glass.

Beating on vehicles.

It turned into a full-blown melee.

My guys managed to get out — but not without getting hurt. Bruises. Contusions. Shaken up badly.

They were lucky.

Very lucky.

That situation could have ended with someone dead.

And the reason it almost did had nothing to do with the park or the gang.

It had everything to do with me.

The Lesson That Landed Hard

Here's the part that matters.

That fight didn't start in the park.

It started at work.

It started with behavior that went unchecked.

With tension that wasn't addressed.

With a boss who didn't step in early enough.

When leaders don't confront small problems, they don't disappear.

They grow legs.

They leave the building.

And eventually, they get handled by someone else.

Usually in a way you don't like.

Why Bosses Must Step In Early

I learned something critical from that moment:

If I don't handle conflict inside the company, the world will handle it for me.

And the world doesn't care about fairness, safety, or long-term consequences.

That was the last time I ever believed that "they'll work it out themselves" was a leadership strategy.

Because what started as trash talk almost turned into a tragedy.

What This Story Proves

This isn't a story about fighting.

It's a story about responsibility.

Small issues deserve immediate attention.

Early confrontation prevents catastrophic outcomes.

And protecting your people sometimes means protecting them from themselves.

Leadership doesn't start when things explode.

It starts when they're still manageable.

The Fear of Letting Go

The hardest part of this phase wasn't learning new skills.

It was letting go of old ones.

I knew how to outwork problems. I didn't yet know how to **design them out**.

Recently I made two very hard and huge decisions for my company.

Changing my logo after 30 years and changing my CRM software after 15 years.

My logo was a top hat and brush that paid homage to the way I started the chimney company. The original kit I bought came with brushes, a couple of tools, a vacuum, a manual on how to do it and most importantly a top hat for marketing.

It was well branded, all over my trucks, trailers, buildings, clothes. . . everything but It wasn't who we are any more.

The logo made us look like chimney sweeps and now chimney sweeping was only 7% of revenue.

We were a specialty contractor that focused on fire and chimney safety. Hard to do but totally necessary to move forward with better messaging.

My CRM (Customer Relationship Management) software was really getting old. We had a million work arounds to get what we needed, it was cheap, it was like a comfy blanket with a few holes in it. I did demos of all types of products and everything promised to be so much more amazing than our aging software but when we really got into it, each one didn't fix all the problems, had hidden issues, was expensive.

Two years ago I realized how far behind we were getting and I had to make the very hard and expensive decision to move.

It totally sucked and sucked harder than I ever imagined but it was the right decision and gets better all of the time. It has also put us on equal footing for all of the new things that are being developed.

I was afraid that if I made these changes, something would break.

The truth was, things were already breaking — just quietly, behind the scenes of we just didn't know what we were missing

What I Had to Admit

This was the admission that finally changed everything:

My effort and comfort was preventing the business from maturing.

As long as I jumped in:

- systems didn't get built
- people didn't grow
- accountability stayed fuzzy

I wasn't protecting the business. I was **propping it up**.

And propped-up businesses collapse the moment the support moves.

The Shift From Hustle to Structure

The shift didn't happen overnight.

It started with small, uncomfortable changes.

Writing things down that lived in my head. Letting people struggle a little longer before stepping in. Allowing imperfect decisions instead of perfect delays.

At first, it felt like things got worse.

More mistakes. More questions. More friction from employees and managers.

People made sure I knew that they liked the old way more, the old way wouldn't have been an issue.

That's normal.

That's what happens when effort steps back and reality steps forward.

What Emerged When I Stopped Being Everywhere

Slowly, something else happened.

People started solving problems without me. Leaders began

to form opinions. Decisions got made faster — not always better, but faster.

And faster decisions meant faster learning.

That's when I realized something important:

Clarity Beats Effort Every Time.

Clear roles beat heroic saves. Clear authority beats constant involvement. Clear systems beat personal sacrifice.

The Emotional Cost No One Talks About

Letting go wasn't just operational.

It was emotional.

I had to separate my worth from my workload. My value from my visibility. My leadership from my presence.

That was harder than any long day or late night.

But it was necessary.

My mentor John Merideth taught me the way to break from it. He said " the business you will really love is the one that doesn't need you.

He said just go away for a week and don't handle problems when you are gone, don't "check in" and when you return, make note of all the problems they had or answers they needed. Make these answers easy to find or known by all. Then go away two weeks and more. The weird thing is he got so good at it that it felt bad when he got back because no one needed him for answers.

In some ways he felt like he lost his identity in the business, in another way, he had built the best company with his leadership and product that was going to be fine without him.

That's the ultimate end for the best boss.

Looking Back With Honesty

If I'm honest, I stayed in the effort phase longer than I should have.

Not because I didn't know better.

Because effort felt safe.

Structure felt risky.

Structure meant admitting I couldn't do it all anymore — and shouldn't.

The Lesson That Lasted

Here's the truth I carry now:

- When effort stops working, it's not a failure. It's an invitation.
- Can you give an example of that principle?
- An invitation to build something stronger than yourself.

If your business still only moves when you push it, that's not leadership — that's leverage waiting to be built.

Why This Matters for What Comes Next

Everything that follows in this book — standards, training, accountability, systems, delegation — only works if you accept this first:

- You cannot outwork complexity.
- You must simplify it as much as possible.

Steve Jobs famously believed that "Simple can be harder than complex," arguing that immense effort must be put into cleaning up thinking to create true simplicity. He believed this, however, was worth it because it allows one to "move mountains." Jobs defined design not just by how it looks, but by how it works

And that moment — when effort finally fails you — isn't the end of something. It's the beginning of real leadership.

THE LEADERSHIP PRINCIPLES

1. Busy does not mean effective.
2. Leaders slow growth when they rescue too often.
3. Systems learn slower than people.
4. Scaling requires tolerance for mistakes.
5. Independence is built, not assumed.

THE VIDEO YOU SHOULD RECORD

Title: **"Why I Stopped Saving the Day"**

Explain:

- Why rescuing people feels productive.
- How it limits growth.
- What mistakes you now allow.
- How you coach instead of fix.

THREE THINGS TO DO THIS WEEK

1. Identify one problem you keep fixing personally.
2. Let someone else handle it — and support them afterward.
3. Document the mistake so the system learns.

CHAPTER 5

Clarity Is Kindness

For a long time, I thought clarity was optional.

I believed good people would "figure it out." I believed intentions mattered more than instructions. I believed that being flexible made me a better boss.

What I didn't realize was that **my flexibility felt like abandonment to the people who worked for me.**

Good people don't need motivation. They need direction.

And when direction is missing, confusion fills the space.

When Good People Start Guessing

There was a stretch where we had talented, hardworking technicians who were genuinely trying to do the right thing — and still missing the mark.

Jobs took too long. Quality varied wildly. Customers got different experiences depending on who showed up.

When I dug into it, I didn't find laziness.

I found guessing.

People were guessing what "good enough" meant. Guessing how much time they were supposed to spend. Guessing when to push back and when to say yes.

And they were guessing because **I hadn't been clear.**

The Lie I Believed About Clarity

I used to believe that clarity boxed people in.

That if I spelled everything out, I'd crush initiative.

That too many rules would kill culture.

That strong people didn't need their hand held.

That belief sounded mature.

It was wrong.

What it actually did was create anxiety.

Because when expectations aren't clear, people don't feel free — they feel exposed.

Story One: The Customer Who Called Me Directly

I remember a customer calling me after a job and saying something that stuck with me:

"I love your company. I love most of your guys. But this last one didn't fit."

That sentence bothered me more than a complaint ever had.

Not because the technician was bad — but because the customer could *feel* inconsistency.

That's when I realized something uncomfortable:

Culture isn't what you say.

It's what people experience when you're not there.

And experience comes from clarity — not intention.

When Flexibility Turns Into Favoritism

Another unintended consequence of unclear expectations showed up internally.

Some technicians were getting more leeway than others.

Some were "trusted."

Some were corrected.

Not because they were treated differently on purpose — but because nothing was written down.

I thought I was being fair.

What the team saw was inconsistency.

And inconsistency erodes trust faster than almost any-thing else.

Story Two: "If You Didn't Write It Down, It Didn't Happen"

One of the most important operational rules we ever adopted came from embarrassment.

A job went sideways.

Details weren't documented.

Work that had been discussed wasn't written down.

When it was questioned later, there was no proof it had ever been addressed.

That's when we adopted a rule that still stands:

If you didn't write it down, it didn't happen.

At first, people thought it was nitpicky.

It wasn't.

It was protective.

It protected technicians.

It protected customers.

It protected the company.

And it removed guessing.

Clarity Protects the People Doing It Right

The biggest myth about clarity is that it's for under-performers.

It's not.

Clarity protects your best people.

High performers want to know:

- where the line is
- what winning looks like
- how they're measured

When those answers are fuzzy, your best people either burn out or leave.

Not because the work is hard — but because the environment is exhausting.

Story Three: The Day Someone Finally Said It Out Loud

One of my better people finally pulled me aside and said:

"Mark, we're not asking you to be harsher.

We're asking you to be clearer."

That sentence hit harder than any complaint.

Because I realized I'd been confusing kindness with ambiguity.

Avoiding clarity didn't make me nicer.

It made me harder to trust.

Why Clear Expectations Feel Uncomfortable at First

Clarity forces commitment.

Once expectations are clear:

- excuses don't work,
- stories fall apart,
- accountability becomes unavoidable.

That's uncomfortable — especially for the boss.

Because clarity removes your ability to explain things away later.

But it also creates stability.

The Shift That Changed Everything

When we finally started writing things down:

- job expectations
- time standards
- quality benchmarks
- communication rules

Something surprising happened.

People relaxed.

They stopped guessing.

They stopped checking every move.

They started owning outcomes.

Because clarity gave them something solid to stand on.

What I Understand Now

Clarity is not control.

Clarity is compassion.

It tells people:

- "This is what good looks like."
- "This is how you win."
- "This is where the line is."

And it gives them dignity by not making them guess.

The Lesson That Lasted

If people are confused, the system is broken — not the person.

And if the system is broken, that's on the boss.

Clarity isn't optional leadership behavior.

It's foundational.

Why This Chapter Matters

Everything that comes next — standards, training, accountability — collapses without clarity.

You cannot enforce what you haven't defined.

And you cannot protect good people if you won't draw clear lines.

Looking Back Honestly

I wish I'd learned this earlier.

I thought I was being patient.

I thought I was being understanding.

I was being vague.

And vagueness costs good people first.

The Truth I Carry Now

If clarity feels uncomfortable, it's probably overdue.

And if you're worried that clear expectations will push people away — they will.

The wrong ones.

The right ones will finally know how to win.

THE LEADERSHIP PRINCIPLES

1. **Vagueness hurts your best people first.** High performers don't need motivation — they need clear expectations so they can win.

2. **Clarity is not harsh — it's humane.** Making people guess feels kind in the moment but creates anxiety over time.

3. **Flexibility without structure becomes favoritism.** When rules live in your head instead of on paper, trust erodes.

4. **If it isn't written down, it didn't happen.** Documentation protects everyone — especially the people doing the job right.

5. **You can't enforce what you haven't defined.** Accountability without clarity is unfair. Clarity always comes first.

THE VIDEO YOU SHOULD RECORD

Record a **5–7 minute video** answering this question:

"What does 'doing a great job' actually look like here?"

In the video:

- Explain what *winning* looks like in your company.
- Define 3–5 non-negotiable standards.
- Clarify where flexibility exists — and where it doesn't.
- Say explicitly: *"If this isn't clear, that's on me — ask."*

This video becomes:

- Onboarding clarity
- A culture anchor
- A reference point when things drift

It also forces **you** to get clear before expecting anyone else to be.

THREE THINGS TO DO THIS WEEK

1. **Write down one expectation you've been assuming instead of stating.** If you've said, "They should know this," that's your clue.

2. **Ask one trusted employee:** "What feels unclear about how we define 'good' around here?"

3. Don't defend. Just listen.

4. **Document one process that currently lives only in your head.** Clarity compounds faster than motivation ever will.

————————————

WHEN EXPECTATIONS
AREN'T CLEAR, PEOPLE
DON'T FEEL FREE
—THEY FEEL EXPOSED.
CLARITY IS NOT CONTROL.
CLARITY IS COMPASSION.

— MARK STONER

————————————

SAFETY,
QUALITY.
TRANSPARENCY

CHAPTER 6

What You Tolerate Becomes the Standard

For years, I believed people's stories.

And because I believed them, they got better at telling them.

Attendance was the issue.

Or at least, that's what it eventually revealed itself to be.

Early on, I didn't think of it as a policy problem. I thought of it as a people problem.

Someone late here. Someone missing a day there. Excuses that sounded reasonable. Emergencies. Flat tires. Sick kids. Bad mornings.

I told myself I was being understanding.

Compassionate.

Human.

What I didn't realize was that I was quietly training my company to operate without standards.

And it took years for the damage to fully show up.

The Stories I Wanted to Believe

In the early days, attendance felt like something that would "work itself out."

I thought if I paid people well, treated them right, and gave them flexibility, they'd naturally respect the schedule. I believed that being harder on attendance would make good people quit.

So when someone was late, I listened to the explanation.

When someone missed a day, I accepted the reason.

When patterns started to form, I told myself I was over-thinking it.

But here's the truth:

- People don't abuse kindness on purpose.
- They drift when boundaries aren't clear.
- And once people realize there's no real consequence, the behavior spreads.

Not because they're bad people.

Because the system allows it.

Monday Chaos

As we grew, the problem grew with us.

Every Monday felt like controlled chaos.

Trucks sitting idle.

Routes being reshuffled.

Good technicians getting sent across town to cover gaps.

Office staff scrambling to call customers and reschedule.

And every single time, the people who paid the price were the ones who showed up.

That's the part I missed for too long.

The problem wasn't the people missing work.

The problem was the people who *were* there — watching me do nothing about it.

Eventually, they started saying it out loud.

"Mark, if you aren't going to stand up for yourself, how can we?"

"Why do I bother being on time?"

"Nothing happens anyway."

That was a punch in the gut.

I had lost credibility — not with my worst people, but with my best ones.

The Moment It Broke

I remember the morning I finally had enough.

Another Monday.

Another call-out.

Another scramble.

I wasn't tired. I was angry.

Not at the people missing work — at myself.

Because I had allowed this to go on for years. I had trained the company to believe attendance was optional if your story was good enough.

That's when it hit me.

If I don't fix this, I'm choosing chaos.

So I stopped negotiating with myself and built a real attendance policy.

The Policy That Changed Everything

I implemented a simple, fair, point-based system.

Not emotional.

Not subjective.

Not personal.

Show up late? Point.

Miss a day without notice? More points.

Stack enough points? Consequence.

No arguing.

No stories.

No exceptions based on likability.

And here's what shocked me—it worked.

Immediately.

Attendance stabilized.

Monday chaos disappeared.

The office calmed down.

The good people relaxed.

Did I lose some people?

Yes.

People I liked.

People I enjoyed.

People who were "mostly" good.

But the company got better fast.

It was probably the single best policy I ever deployed.

Not because it was harsh — but because it was clear.

Why Tolerance Is Leadership Failure

Here's the truth most owners don't want to hear:

Your standards are not what you say.

They're what you tolerate.

You can have policies on paper.

You can give speeches.

You can talk about values all day.

But the company watches what you let slide.

And they adjust accordingly.

The Turning Point

When I finally enforced attendance standards, something unexpected happened.

Morale went up.

Not because people loved rules — but because they trusted the system.

The people who wanted structure stayed.

The people who wanted flexibility without account-ability left.

And for the first time in a long time, the company felt predictable again.

Predictability is peace.

What This Chapter Is Actually About

This chapter isn't about attendance.

It's about leadership courage.

It's about choosing short-term discomfort over long-term chaos.

It's about protecting your good people.

It's about understanding that kindness without standards isn't kindness at all.

THE LEADERSHIP PRINCIPLES

1. What you tolerate becomes the standard — every time.
2. Avoiding confrontation punishes your best people.
3. Standards protect culture, not crush it.
4. Once you know about a problem, you own it.
5. Credibility is earned through consistency, not likability.

THE VIDEO YOU SHOULD RECORD

Record a video titled: **"The Standard We Will Not Compromise"**

In the video:

- Explain *why* attendance (or another core standard) matters.
- Acknowledge past inconsistency.
- Clearly define expectations going forward.
- State consequences calmly and confidently.

This video becomes a cultural reset button.

THREE THINGS TO DO THIS WEEK

1. Identify one behavior you've been tolerating that you shouldn't.
2. Decide what the standard actually is — in writing.
3. Enforce it consistently, even when it's uncomfortable.

Because leadership doesn't fail loudly. It fails slowly — through tolerance.

TRANSPARENCY DOESN'T ELIMINATE PAIN — IT MAKES PAIN SURVIVABLE.

— MARK STONER

CHAPTER 7

Protect Your People

There is a moment every boss faces where avoiding confrontation stops being a personal weakness and starts becoming. For me, it's when a good or even great employee turns toxic. Great people don't always stay great and that shift is always hard for me because I always want them to be great again.

I thought confrontation meant escalation. I thought it meant losing people. I thought it meant things could get heated, emotional, or out of control. I worried I'd say the wrong thing, or get too angry, or make a bad situation worse.

So instead, I stayed calm. Too calm.

I swallowed things I shouldn't have.

I waited longer than I should have.

I told myself problems would work themselves out.

They never do.

The Myth That Confrontation Destroys Teams

Early on, I believed confrontation was risky.

I worried I would:

- Lose a talented employee
- Create drama
- Damage morale
- Escalate conflict

What I didn't understand yet was this:

Avoiding confrontation doesn't eliminate conflict.

It just transfers the cost to your best people.

The worst behavior in any company never hurts the people doing it.

It hurts the people who have to work around it.

The Company That Taught Me the Hard Truth

I was consulting for a company during their busiest season of the year.

They had a key employee — highly talented, extremely productive, and responsible for bringing in a lot of reve-nue. Everyone knew he was difficult. Loud. Demeaning. Aggressive.

People avoided him.

Managers tiptoed around him.

The owners justified it because "he makes us too much money."

Then it crossed a line.

He told the owner's son that he would "kick his dad's ass."

Still, nothing happened.

That's when I finally asked the owner a simple question:

"Is your integrity for sale?"

I explained it plainly.

"If someone brings you enough money, you'll allow them to abuse your people. That's the precedent you're setting."

It hit him hard.

Not because he didn't know it was wrong — but because he had convinced himself it was necessary.

He fired the employee immediately.

And here's what surprised him most:

The company got better almost overnight.

Not more profitable at first — but healthier. Calmer. More focused.

Because the team finally felt protected.

Why Protecting Your People Is a Boss's Job

A boss does not exist to keep everyone happy.

A boss exists to:

- Set the standard,
- Enforce the standard,
- Protect the people who live up to the standard.

When you allow one person to operate above the rules:

- You tell everyone else the rules don't matter,
- You normalize bad behavior,
- You make excellence feel optional.

That's not leadership.

That's abdication.

Nice vs Kind (And Why Bosses Get This Wrong)

There's a concept from the book *Not Nice* that stuck with me.

Nice is avoiding discomfort. Nice is for yourself so people like you. Nice is...selfish.

Kind is doing what's right, even when it's uncomfortable. Kind is always for others.

Nice delays conversations.

Kind has them early.

Nice worries about being liked.

Kind worries about outcomes.

Nice protects feelings.

Kind protects people.

Most bosses think they're being kind when they're actually being nice — and the company pays the price.

I have had this wrong for so long! My thinking was that if I was nice enough to you, you would stay with me. If I held you accountable, you would leave and you wouldn't like working for me.

The Blind Technician

I didn't want to hire him.

That's the honest truth.

He came to me in his early 30s and had advanced macular degeneration. His twin brother had it too. He was already technically blind. If he got extremely close to something he could make out shapes and shadows, but that was about it.

And we run a chimney company.

Ladders. Roofs. Tools. Customers' homes. Liability everywhere.

From a business standpoint it made no sense.

One of my technicians kept pushing me. He said, "I'll take him as my full-time apprentice. I'll stay with him. Just give him a chance."

So we did.

I was nervous. I was worried about safety. I was worried about customers. Mostly, I was worried about responsibility. As an owner you're always doing that quiet calculation — what happens if something goes wrong?

But he just wanted to work.

He didn't want a disability check.

He didn't want sympathy.

He wanted a job.

He was blue collar through and through. He loved working on cars. Loved using his hands. Loved being part of a crew. Every single morning he was happy just to be there.

And then something unexpected happened.

He became one of the best chimney sweepers we had.

Not "good considering his condition."

Good.

Actually better than many guys with full sight.

Because he couldn't rely on vision, he relied on touch. He moved slower. More carefully. More intentionally. He would feel every joint in the liner, every edge in the flue. He was meticulous.

When he finished a chimney, his partner would run the inspection camera afterward for safety verification — and it was spotless. Consistently spotless.

He wasn't working despite his limitation.

He was working differently because of it.

Sometimes I had to send him with other technicians and I'd hear the complaints.

They liked him. Nobody disliked him. But they didn't want the responsibility. It made their day harder. It slowed them down. It added pressure.

And I understood that.

But over time something else happened.

He changed the tone of the shop.

He never complained.

Never had a bad attitude.

Never asked for special treatment.

He was just grateful.

Grateful to work.

Grateful to learn.

Grateful to be part of something.

In a trade where guys could grumble about weather, crawl-spaces, and schedules, he showed up happy just to have the opportunity.

You couldn't ignore that.

There were funny moments too.

One time he was inside a home sweeping a chimney while the other tech was on the roof and night fell while he was working. He didn't use lights because they didn't help him much. The homeowner walked into the room and found him still sweeping — in complete darkness.

They were startled.

He wasn't.

Lights didn't matter to him.

Another time a technician forgot and asked him at an intersection, "You clear on your side?"

He said, "Looks good to me, man."

We laughed about that for a long time.

But underneath the humor was something heavier.

He was losing what most of us depend on every second of the day — and he still showed up wanting to work.

During one of our team meetings he asked if he could say something to the group.

He stood there in front of the technicians and said,

"I just want to thank all of you guys for keeping me safe and letting me work with you. I don't have a lot of options to do much in my life, and I really love working with you all."

The whole room went quiet.

Then my team started tearing up.

These were grown men who worked on roofs and crawlspaces every day, and in that moment nobody cared about schedules, production, or complaints.

I never heard another technician complain about working with him again.

Not once.

Degenerative diseases don't pause.

They progress.

Over time his vision got worse and worse. Eventually it became dangerous for him just to move around a jobsite.

The final moment came at a customer's house when he walked straight into a swimming pool.

That was it.

I knew what I had to do, and it was one of the harder

conversations I've ever had as an owner. Not because he did anything wrong — because he did everything right.

I had to tell a man who wanted to work, who valued the job, and who had earned his place, that I couldn't let him keep doing it.

He took it well.

Better than I did.

We've remained friends.

Watching him changed how I see people.

As owners we deal with performance problems, lateness, complaints, and attitude issues. It's easy to start believing effort is just a choice everyone is making equally.

Then you meet someone carrying a burden they didn't choose — and still bringing more effort and gratitude than people with every advantage.

He never tried to teach anyone a lesson.

But he taught the whole company one anyway.

He taught us grace.

He taught us perspective.

Standards still mattered. Work still mattered. Accountability still mattered.

But compassion mattered too.

A boss must protect the company.

A mature boss remembers he's leading human beings.

That technician didn't lower our standards.

He raised our awareness.

And ever since then, whenever a problem walks into my office, I try to remember something I didn't always know earlier in my career:

You don't always know what someone else is carrying.

My Own Blind Spot

I had to learn this lesson personally.

There were times I let small behaviors slide because I didn't want to deal with them. Little comments. Dismissive attitudes. Passive aggression.

I told myself it wasn't worth the fight.

Meanwhile, my best people were watching.

They were watching me avoid things.

They were watching me rationalize things.

They were watching me choose comfort over clarity.

Eventually, someone said it out loud:

"Why do we have to work around this?"

That's when it hit me.

When you don't protect your people, you force them to protect themselves.

And that's when disengagement begins.

Healthy Confrontation Builds Trust

The best companies don't avoid friction.

They use it.

Healthy confrontation:

- Clears confusion
- Stops resentment
- Reinforces standards
- Builds respect

People don't want a leader who avoids problems.

They want a leader who will step in when things go sideways.

Especially in blue-collar work, where the environments are physical, fast-moving, and unforgiving.

When Knowing Becomes Responsibility

A friend of mine went through something that permanently changed how I think about leadership.

It was one of those stories you never forget — not because it's dramatic, but because it's devastating.

He was a good man. A generous leader. Deeply compassionate. The kind of guy who genuinely wanted the best for people. He even did ministry work in prisons. His heart was always aimed toward grace.

He had a few employees who smoked marijuana.

And here's the part that matters most:

He knew about it.

His posture was understanding. *So what if they smoke pot sometimes?*

He didn't see himself as permissive — he saw himself as kind.

Holding people accountable felt mean to him.

Confrontation felt like punishment.

Grace felt like leadership.

Until one day, everything changed.

The Day Kindness Failed

Two technicians were working on a chimney, standing on scaffolding. Nearby power lines ran closer than they should have.

In a moment that happened faster than anyone could react, electricity arced from the power line.

One of the technicians was electrocuted and killed.

It was horrific.

A life lost.

A family shattered.

A business wrecked.

A leader broken.

There are no words that make that kind of tragedy smaller.

The Consequence No One Expects

What followed made it even worse.

The family sued my friend — not just the company, but him personally.

Their argument was simple and devastating:

"You knew these technicians may have been under the influence.

You knew the work was dangerous.

And you let them do it anyway."

They won.

The settlement was enormous.

And it wasn't just financial.

It changed him forever.

The Lesson That Cannot Be Ignored

This story burned itself into my brain for one reason:

Once you are aware of a problem, **you own it.**

You don't get to un-know it.

You don't get to delay it.

You don't get to call grace leadership and walk away.

If something is illegal, dangerous, or wrong — and you know about it — doing nothing is a decision.

And that decision can make you personally accountable.

Why This Matters for Every Boss

This wasn't a bad man.

This wasn't a careless leader.

This wasn't someone trying to cut corners.

This was someone who confused being *nice* with being *kind.*

Kindness protects people.

Niceness avoids discomfort.

And avoidance, in leadership, has consequences far beyond hurt feelings.

The Responsibility of Knowing

As a boss, you don't just manage outcomes.

You manage risk.

You manage safety.

You manage the moral and legal responsibility of the decisions you allow.

Grace without accountability isn't grace.

It's negligence.

And sometimes the most loving thing you can do is step in early — before the consequences step in for you.

Chaos is dangerous.

Silence is dangerous.

Unclear authority is dangerous.

Correction Works Best When It's Small and Early

One of the most valuable lessons I ever learned came from training Shetland Sheepdogs for show.

In dog training, correction has to be:

- Quick
- Small
- Immediate

You don't let the dog wander ten feet off course and then yank the leash and yell.

You make a short correction *before* the behavior escalates.

Leadership works the same way.

Small, early corrections prevent big, emotional confrontations later.

When you wait:

- Problems grow.
- Emotions harden.
- Stakes increase.

Confrontation doesn't get easier with time.

It gets heavier.

The Freedom of Protecting Your Good People

Once I truly committed to protecting the team, something unexpected happened.

Leadership became easier.

Not because there were fewer problems — but because I stopped negotiating with myself about whether to act.

When people knew I would step in:

- Gossip dropped.
- Tension decreased.
- Standards stabilized.

Good people relax when they know someone has their back.

Bad behavior hates sunlight.

What This Chapter Is Really About

This chapter is not about being aggressive.

It's about being responsible.

Being the boss means:

- You absorb discomfort so your team doesn't have to.
- You confront early so others can focus on their work.
- You draw lines so people know where they stand.

Avoidance is easy.

Protection takes courage.

THE LEADERSHIP PRINCIPLES

1. Avoiding confrontation shifts the burden to your best people.
2. Nice avoids discomfort; kind addresses reality.
3. One protected bad actor damages the whole culture.
4. Early, small corrections prevent big blowups.
5. Trust is built when people know you'll step in.

THE VIDEO YOU SHOULD RECORD

Record a video titled:

"How We Handle Conflict Here"

In the video:

- Explain your philosophy on confrontation.
- Clarify that issues will be addressed early and respectfully.
- State that protecting the team is non-negotiable.
- Reinforce that standards apply to everyone.

This video sets the tone for psychological safety and accountability.

THREE THINGS TO DO THIS WEEK

1. Identify one behavior you've been avoiding addressing.
2. Have the conversation early — calm, direct, and specific.

3. Tell your team what you expect them to bring to you
    — and what you'll handle.

Because the best teams don't need less leadership.

They need leaders willing to step in.

GRACE WITHOUT ACCOUNTABILITY ISN'T GRACE. IT'S NEGLIGENCE.

— MARK STONER

CHAPTER 8

Training Isn't Netflix

There's a lie we tell ourselves in blue-collar businesses because it makes us feel efficient.

We tell ourselves that certification equals readiness.

Pass the test.

Get the patch.

Put them in a truck.

And for a long time, I believed that lie too.

The Big Dog / Little Dog Trap

We didn't call it that at the time, but looking back, that's exactly what it was.

A new technician would ride with a senior tech. The senior tech was good — fast, confident, experienced. The new guy would help where needed. Carry tools. Set ladders. Lay tarps. Clean up.

From the outside, it looked like training.

But it wasn't.

The "big dog" did the thinking.

The "little dog" did the helping.

No explanation.

No decision-making.

No customer conversations.

No real reps.

They weren't learning how to do the job.

They were learning how to stay busy.

And busy feels productive — until it isn't.

The Moment It Hit Me In the Face

The moment this system broke open for me came from my son.

He had helped us every summer since he was fourteen. He worked with different crews all through college. He knew the guys. He knew the tools. He knew the culture.

After graduation, he hadn't landed a job in his field yet, so he came to work for us full-time and became a certified technician.

The certification part was easy for him.

Running a service truck was not.

He struggled. He hated it. He was frustrated. Customers were frustrated. His confidence dropped fast.

Then one day, he came to me and said something that really stuck with me.

"Dad, I don't know what I'm doing."

That wasn't an excuse. That was clarity.

He explained it plainly.

"I've never actually learned how to run jobs. I handed guys tools. I set up ladders. I cleaned up job sites. I sat in the truck while they talked to customers. I passed a test, but I wasn't trained."

He was right.

And that one sentence forced me to look at my entire operation honestly.

Certification Didn't Fail — Leadership Did

This wasn't about intelligence.

My son is incredibly smart. He seeks answers before acting. He looks for gaps. I tend to act first and learn the lesson second. That contrast was exactly what I needed.

He wasn't failing because he lacked ability.

He was failing because we hadn't prepared him.

And when I looked deeper, I realized something uncomfortable:

He wasn't the only one.

We were certifying people and calling them "ready" when they weren't.

And the consequences showed up everywhere:

- Late jobs
- Overcomplicated inspections
- Missed appointments
- Canceled calls
- Frustrated customers
- Burned-out technicians

Training gaps always show up downstream.

Why "Ride-Along" Training Fails

Ride-along training fails because it assumes proximity equals learning.

It doesn't.

Learning requires:

- Explanation
- Repetition
- Context
- Feedback

- Responsibility

Without structure, ride-alongs turn into observation.

And observation without responsibility builds false confidence.

People think they know more than they do — until they're alone.

When Pressure Exposes Weak Training

The worst part wasn't mistakes.

The worst part was confidence erosion.

When a technician finds things others didn't, customers get confused.

When appointments run long, trust erodes.

When jobs get canceled because someone ran out of time, credibility disappears.

And that pressure lands hardest on the person least equipped to carry it.

That's not fair to them.

That's a leadership failure.

Building a Real Apprenticeship

Around this same time, we were starting a chimney franchise with partners. We needed a system for franchisees, and I needed one desperately for Ashbusters.

So we stopped pretending certification was enough and built a real apprenticeship program.

Five stages.

Clear timelines.

Real expectations.

Day 1–30

Day 31–60

Day 61–90

Day 90–120

Each phase includes:

- Safety
- SOPs
- Code language
- Customer communication
- Real-world scenarios

New hires spend roughly two weeks in classroom training.

Then they continue structured online learning while riding with technicians — but now with defined outcomes.

They don't just watch.

They explain.

They decide.

They lead parts of the job.

Before anyone runs a truck alone, they:

- Pass certification.
- Ride with a head trainer.
- Demonstrate readiness.

Not confidence.

Competence.

A lot of this work now lives inside SureFire Training Academy — but it started as a painful internal lesson.

Training Is Not Entertainment

Here's another truth owners don't like to say out loud:

Training is hard.

It requires focus.

It requires effort.

It requires repetition.

This isn't Netflix.

There are quizzes.

There are expectations.

There is accountability.

Some people don't like that.

That's okay.

Because if someone won't invest in learning the job, they won't survive doing the job.

What This Chapter Is Really About

This chapter isn't about apprenticeships.

It's about honesty.

Honesty about readiness.

Honesty about gaps.

Honesty about what we're actually teaching — versus what we assume people are learning.

Good people fail in bad systems.

And certification without training is a bad system.

THE LEADERSHIP PRINCIPLES

- Certification does not equal readiness.
- Ride-alongs without structure create false confidence.
- Training gaps always surface under pressure.
- Apprenticeships protect both customers and technicians.
- Leadership owns readiness — not the individual.

THE VIDEO YOU SHOULD RECORD

Record a video titled: **"Why Certification Isn't Enough Here"**

In the video:

- Explain the difference between passing a test and being ready.
- Outline your training stages.
- Set expectations for effort and accountability.
- Say clearly: *"We will not rush readiness."*

This video saves you years of frustration.

THREE THINGS TO DO THIS WEEK

1. Identify one role where certification is being mistaken for readiness.
2. Define what "ready" actually means — in writing.
3. Add structure to one training step that currently relies on observation.

Because untrained confidence is dangerous. And training done right is one of the most respectful things a boss can do.

CHAPTER 9

When Confidence Isn't Competence

Some hiring mistakes don't show up on paper.

They show up in the room.

I learned that lesson the hard way with a guy my team eventually nicknamed *Grand Daddy Long Legs*.

The Hire That Should Have Worked

He called me out of the blue.

He said he was relocating to Nashville and wanted to work for "a world-class company like yours." That should've been my first pause. Compliments have a way of sneaking past discernment.

When he came in for the interview, he looked the part. Dressed a little too nice for our trade. Older than I expected. Tall. Silver hair. Confident — very confident.

He knew the code book inside and out. Quoted sections

effortlessly. Told great stories. Had run his own company before and said he was tired of the stress and just wanted to work for someone else.

On paper, he was exactly what my young company needed.

Experience. Authority. Confidence.

I thought I had found gold.

My wife didn't like him from the jump.

She couldn't fully articulate it — just a gut feeling. Something was off.

I ignored it.

That was mistake number one.

The Room Felt It Before I Did

My technicians hated him almost immediately.

They said he had an air of superiority. He talked *at* people, not *with* them. Every job turned into a production. Too complex. Too slow. Too dramatic.

The office staff felt creeped out. He dismissed their input. Touched shoulders when talking. Made people uncomfortable without ever doing anything "technically" wrong.

Then a customer called.

"I love you and your guys," she said. "But this guy doesn't fit."

That should have been the end of it.

Instead, I rationalized.

"He just needs time."

"They'll adjust."

"He's experienced — they're young."

I confused authority with leadership.

Knowledge with trust.

Confidence with competence.

When Credentials Become Camouflage

Every job he touched turned into a mess.

Jobs ran long.

Appointments were missed.

Customers were frustrated.

He "found" things other techs hadn't — which didn't build confidence, it created doubt.

Instead of elevating the team, he destabilized it.

And slowly, quietly, I started hearing things about his reputation where he used to live.

Burned bridges.

Conflict.

A pattern I should've seen earlier.

The signs were there from day one.

I just didn't want to see them.

Why This One Hurt

This wasn't a bad hire because he lacked skill.

It was a bad hire because he lacked humility.

And humility matters more than experience every single time.

My biggest mistake wasn't hiring him.

It was ignoring the signals.

My wife felt it.

My team felt it.

My customers felt it.

I overruled all of them because I wanted him to work.

That's not leadership. **That's ego.**

Being Wrong Is Not Failure

Here's something I've learned the hard way:

You're going to be wrong about people.

A lot.

That's not failure.

That's leadership.

Failure is refusing to admit it.

Failure is protecting your pride instead of your people.

Failure is doubling down when the evidence is clear.

It took me too long to correct this one, and the cost wasn't just money — it was trust.

The Difference Between Presence and Performance

Some people perform well in interviews.

They speak confidently.

They sound experienced.

They know the language.

But presence is revealed in:

- How people feel around them.
- Whether teams relax or tense up.
- Whether customers feel safe or uneasy.
- Whether problems calm down or multiply.

You can't teach presence.

You can't certify humility.

And you can't fake cultural fit for long.

What This Chapter Is Really About

This chapter isn't about one bad hire.

It's about learning to listen.

To your gut.

To your spouse.

To your team.

To your customers.

Because leadership is not about being right all the time.

It's about correcting fast when you're wrong.

THE LEADERSHIP PRINCIPLES

- Confidence is not the same as competence.
- Experience without humility destabilizes teams.
- Your team feels cultural mismatches before you do.
- Customers notice fit faster than owners.
- Being wrong about people is inevitable — not acting is optional.

THE VIDEO YOU SHOULD RECORD

Record a video titled: **"What We Look for Beyond Resumes"**

In the video:

- Talk about cultural fit.
- Explain why humility matters more than experience.
- Share how feedback flows upward.
- Say clearly: *"If you make the room worse, you won't stay."*

This video saves you from repeating this mistake.

THREE THINGS TO DO THIS WEEK

1. Think about one hire that "should have worked" but didn't — why?
2. Ask your team who makes their job easier and who makes it harder.
3. Commit to acting faster when the signals are clear.

Because leadership isn't about proving you're right. It's about protecting the people who rely on you to be honest.

CHAPTER 10

Standards Aren't Optional

I was bad at spotting drug use.

Not because I was careless.

Because I was naïve.

I had never done drugs. I didn't grow up around them. I didn't understand how common they were in the workforce, especially in physically demanding blue-collar trades. For a long time, I assumed that if you paid people well, treated them fairly, and respected them, they would naturally make good decisions.

That belief almost got someone killed. And it almost wrecked my company.

The Injury That Changed Everything

The moment that woke me up didn't start with drugs. It started with blood.

One of our technicians was installing a chimney liner and suffered a deep, serious cut. Not a scratch. Not something you shake off. This was the kind of injury that clearly required medical attention.

I told him, "You need to go to the hospital."

He refused.

That's when my stomach dropped.

At first, I didn't understand why someone would do that. Then it hit me. He didn't want to be tested. He didn't want a drug screen. He didn't want what came next.

That was the first time I realized how exposed we really were.

Not just legally.

Morally.

Operationally.

Soon after, I learned something about our workers' comp policy that scared the hell out of me. If an employee tested positive for drugs after an accident, the claim would not be paid. That meant medical bills. Lawsuits. Families without support. And a company holding the bag for something that could have been prevented.

Up until that point, I had believed something dangerously wrong: that being good to people would automatically result in people being good in return.

That's not how reality works.

When Employees Had to Tell Me the Truth

The next lesson was even more humbling.

I wasn't the one who discovered the drug use.

My employees did.

Good employees came to me quietly and said, "Mark, this is happening."

They knew before I did. They saw it every day. They also saw that nothing was being done about it.

That realization was brutal.

Because when leadership doesn't act, it sends a message — even if it's unintentional.

The message wasn't that drugs were allowed.

The message was that standards were negotiable.

And that message cost us in ways that didn't show up on a P&L.

Trust eroded. Workmanship declined.

Resentment grew among the people who showed up clear-headed and ready to work every day.

The people doing the right thing felt unprotected.

That's when I finally understood something fundamental:

Standards don't exist unless they are enforced.

The "Crack Is Cocaine" Moment

Not long after that, I had a situation that perfectly illustrated how disconnected I had been from reality.

A technician had been missing work. Showing up late. Acting strange. Everything about his behavior raised red flags. I finally sent him for a drug test.

The results came back positive for cocaine.

The next day, I brought him into my office to let him go. I told him the test came back positive.

He looked me straight in the eye and said,

"For what?"

I said, "Cocaine."

He was adamant.

"No way. I've never done cocaine. Ever."

He was convincing. Passionate, even. For a moment, I almost questioned myself.

Then I said, "Well. . . crack is cocaine."

He froze.

He looked down.

Paused.

Then quietly said, "Oh. . . well I guess it's right."

That was the end of his employment.

That moment stuck with me, not because it was funny — though it was — but because it exposed how far removed I had been from the reality my company was operating in.

I wasn't leading with standards.

I was reacting to problems after they escalated.

This drives home a truth most owners don't want to face:

Once you are made aware of a problem, you own it.

You don't get to unknow what you know.

You don't get to delay responsibility.

And you don't get to hide behind good intentions.

Acting Is Leadership

After that, everything changed for me.

We implemented drug testing at three levels:

- Pre-employment
- Random
- For cause

It wasn't popular. It wasn't comfortable. And marijuana became the hardest issue as laws changed.

We made a clear decision. You cannot be under the influence on the job. Period. If marijuana showed up on a test, it wasn't automatic termination — but every other drug was.

The point wasn't punishment.

The point was protection.

Protection of customers.

Protection of coworkers.

Protection of families.

Protection of the business itself.

And here's what surprised me most: the good people were relieved.

They wanted standards. They wanted to know the company had their back. They wanted leadership to do what leadership is supposed to do.

THE LEADERSHIP PRINCIPLE

Standards aren't personal.

They're not about control.

They're not about ego.

They're not about being "hard."

They are about safety, trust, and responsibility.

Being kind doesn't mean being permissive.

Being nice doesn't mean being negligent.

A boss who refuses to act is not compassionate.

They are dangerous.

WHAT THIS CHAPTER IS REALLY ABOUT

This chapter isn't about drugs.

It's about action.

It's about understanding that every time you delay enforcing a standard, you are making a decision — whether you admit it or not.

You are choosing chaos over clarity.

Stories over systems.

Risk over responsibility.

And the longer you wait, the higher the cost.

THREE THINGS TO DO THIS WEEK

1. **Write down your non-negotiables.** If someone
    violates them, what happens? If you can't answer
    that clearly, the standard doesn't exist.

2. **Act on the next issue immediately.** Not emotionally.
    Not aggressively. Immediately.

3. **Protect your good people.** Every time you don't, you
    tell them they're on their own.

That's not leadership.

Standards aren't optional. They're the foundation.

IF YOUR BUSINESS
DEPENDS ON YOU,
YOU DON'T OWN A
BUSINESS—YOU HAVE A JOB.
AND IT'S THE WORST JOB
IN THE WORLD BECAUSE
YOU'RE WORKING FOR A
LUNATIC!

— MICHEAL GERBER, THE E-MYTH

CHAPTER 11

You're Not Broke — You're Just Guessing

Early in my career, I ran my business by looking at one thing, the bank account.

If there was money in it, I felt good.

If there wasn't, I felt sick.

That was the extent of my financial system.

No budget.

No cash flow statement.

No real understanding of where money came from, where it went, or when it was supposed to arrive.

Just vibes.

For a while, that worked. Or at least it felt like it did. When you're small, chaos is disguised as hustle. You can outwork mistakes. You can patch problems. You can stay late and fix what breaks.

But there's a moment in every growing business where guessing stops working.

And when that moment hits, it hits hard.

Running Blind at Scale

I remember thinking we were doing great. Revenue was up. Phones were ringing. Trucks were rolling. From the outside, everything looked healthy.

Then payroll hit.

Then taxes came due.

Then equipment broke.

And suddenly, the business that felt "successful" was gasping for air.

I wasn't broke. I was blind.

I didn't understand cash flow. I didn't understand timing. I didn't understand how quickly growth can starve a business if it isn't managed.

Money was coming in — but not when it needed to. Expenses were going out — faster than I realized. And I had no real visibility into how close I was to the edge.

That's when I learned a hard truth most owners avoid:

Revenue doesn't pay bills. Cash flow does.

The Danger of the Checking-Account CEO

I see this constantly when I talk to other business owners.

They'll say, "We're doing about five million a year,"
with pride.

Then they'll admit they can't sleep at night.

Then they'll admit payroll scares them every two weeks.

That disconnect always points to the same thing.

They're running their company by checking their balance
instead of understanding their business.

A bank account is a snapshot.

It is not a system.

It is not a strategy.

When you don't understand cash flow, every decision feels
emotional. Every downturn feels personal. Every expense
feels threatening.

And that fear leaks into leadership.

You hesitate.

You delay.

You guess.

Why Secrecy Creates Fiction

When owners don't talk about money, employees make up stories.

They assume the owner is getting rich on their labor.

They assume margins are massive.

They assume there's money being hidden somewhere.

Almost none of that is true.

But silence invites fiction.

I learned that the hard way.

When we started opening the books — explaining margins, overhead, reinvestment, risk — something shifted.

People stopped guessing.

They started asking better questions.

The tone changed from, "Why do they get that?"

to, "How does this actually work?"

That's when alignment starts.

Financial Clarity Creates Leadership Calm

The biggest gift understanding cash flow gave me wasn't profit.

It was calm.

When you know:

- what you need to make,
- when you need to make it,
- what happens if you don't.

You stop panicking.

You stop reacting emotionally.

You start leading.

Calm leadership isn't passive.

It's informed.

And informed leadership is impossible without financial clarity.

Guessing Feels Safer Than Knowing — Until It Isn't

Here's the uncomfortable truth.

Many owners don't want clarity.

They'd rather guess than confront reality.

They'd rather hope than measure.

They'd rather feel busy than feel accountable.

Because numbers don't care how hard you work.

They just tell the truth.

But avoiding the truth doesn't protect you. It delays the reckoning.

And when it comes, it's louder.

THE LEADERSHIP PRINCIPLES

You're not broke.

You're guessing.

And guessing is not a strategy.

A boss who understands cash flow can make hard decisions early — when they're still manageable. A boss who doesn't understand it waits until options disappear.

Financial literacy isn't about spreadsheets.

It's about responsibility.

THREE THINGS TO DO THIS WEEK

1. **Stop running your business from the bank account.** Learn where cash actually comes from and when it leaves.

2. **Explain the money to your team.** Not everything — but enough to replace rumor with reality.

3. **Make one decision based on numbers, not fear.** Calm follows clarity.

CHAPTER 12

Where I Don't Have to Be the Boss

I've always been good at carrying things.

Tools. Ladders. Chimney liners. Responsibility.

The business started small enough that if something went wrong, it was me. Customer mad? Me. Employee late? Me. Truck broke? Me. Cash short? Definitely me.

In the early days I thought that was what being a business owner meant — being available to everything and everyone at all times.

And for a long time, it worked.

I could outwork most problems.

What I didn't understand was this:

You can outwork problems. . . but you can't outcarry pressure forever.

Because leadership doesn't stay at the office.

It rides home in the truck with you.

I used to pull into the driveway still mid-conversation in my head.

An employee said something.

A customer was upset.

Payroll was tight.

A decision didn't feel right.

I'd shut the truck door, walk into the house, and physically I was home — but mentally I was still on a roof somewhere.

I'd sit at dinner and barely hear half of what was said.

Not because I didn't care.

Because my brain was still working.

I thought that was dedication.

It wasn't.

It was overflow.

My wife, Terry never tried to be part of the business.

She didn't want to manage employees.

She didn't want to help run operations.

She didn't want a role in decisions. And that ended up being one of the most important parts of my leadership.

She taught me something I didn't understand for years.

Men need cave time.

Not escape. Not avoidance.

Quiet.

After a full day of decisions, conversations, conflict, and problem solving, I just didn't have anything left to say. I wasn't upset. I wasn't withdrawn. I was empty.

I had used all my words.

Leadership is constant talking, constant processing, constant evaluating. By the end of the day my battery was out.

Terry understood that before I did.

She didn't press me with questions. She didn't need a report. She didn't need me to keep performing.

She'd just ask, "How was your day?"

Sometimes I'd answer.

Sometimes I'd just sit.

And she let me.

That quiet was recovery.

Employees see the boss giving direction.

Customers see the boss giving reassurance.

Managers see the boss giving answers.

Nobody sees the part where the boss doesn't have answers.

You make decisions without certainty far more than people realize.

You hire hoping.

You expand hoping.

You promise stability hoping.

Confidence is part of the job, even when certainty isn't.

You carry pressure quietly because you have to.

And you need somewhere safe to set it down.

For me, that wasn't a meeting, a hobby, or a vacation.

It was a house where nobody needed me to lead.

There were seasons the business was heavy.

Times I didn't know how payroll would work.

Times employees were mad at me.

Times decisions hurt people I cared about.

I'd walk through the door and the house was calm. No performance needed. No explanation required.

THE LEADERSHIP PRINCIPLES

Respect is not demanded.

It's demonstrated.

People don't need you to be perfect.

They need you to be consistent.

They need to know:

- where the line is,
- that it won't move,
- that you'll act when it's crossed.

That's not being harsh.

That's being a boss.

THREE THINGS TO DO THIS WEEK

1. **Identify one issue you've been calm about for too long.** Calm is only leadership when it's paired with action.
2. **Have the conversation early.** Small corrections prevent big consequences.
3. **Choose respect over comfort.** Your team doesn't need you to be liked. They need you to lead.

CHAPTER 13

Being Wrong Isn't Failure

One of the most damaging things we learn early in life has nothing to do with business.

It's school.

From the time we're kids, we're taught that success and failure live on opposite ends of the spectrum. You get an A or you get an F. One means you're smart. The other means you're not. One moves you forward. The other sends you backward.

That framework is completely backwards for business.

In the real world, A's and F's live on the same side of the equation.

If you want to build something meaningful—something that lasts—you're going to be wrong. A lot. And being wrong is not failure. Refusing to learn from it is.

It took me years to understand that.

The Hire I Almost Missed Completely

Jonah did not impress us in his interview.

In fact, if I'm being honest, my first impression was that he was a punk kid. Young. Rough around the edges. Not polished. Not particularly confident in the way that makes owners feel comfortable.

If I had trusted my instincts alone, I might have passed.

What I didn't see in that moment was what mattered most.

Inside Jonah was a strong leader. But it wasn't loud. It wasn't obvious. And it wasn't trying to impress anyone. It just needed opportunity—and direction.

Once he was in the company, something started to show up.

He cared. He asked questions. He took responsibility. When things broke, he didn't deflect—he owned it. When people struggled, he leaned in instead of away.

Leadership didn't arrive all at once. It developed.

Today, Jonah runs our Knoxville division. He's a key leader in the company. Calm. Trusted. Respected. The kind of leader people follow because they know he'll do the right thing when it's hard.

If I had been unwilling to be wrong about my first impression, I would have missed one of the best leaders in my organization.

When People Outgrow the Role You Hired Them For

Ray's story surprised me in a different way.

I hired Ray for finance. That was it. I wasn't looking for a partner. I wasn't looking for a confidant. I certainly wasn't expecting a deep leadership relationship.

If you'd asked me then whether we'd become close, I would have laughed.

And yet, over time, Ray started showing something I hadn't anticipated.

He thought in systems. He saw around corners. He brought structure where I brought instinct. He asked questions that made the business stronger—not just cleaner on paper.

More importantly, he cared about doing it right.

Leadership showed up not because I planned for it—but because I paid attention when it emerged.

Ray is now my Vice President. Not because that was the plan. But because the business needed it—and he earned it.

That experience taught me something critical:

You are going to be wrong about people.

Sometimes you'll overestimate them.

Sometimes you'll underestimate them.

Neither is failure—unless you refuse to adjust.

Buying Mistakes Is the Cost of Growth

I have a saying I've used for years, usually half-joking, but always true:

"To build a large company, you have to buy a lot of mistakes—and take responsibility for some crappy work."

That's not pessimism. That's reality.

New technicians and employees HAVE to make mistakes and sometimes huge ones with extra zeros on the end. The way you react is everything. If you are hard to make mistakes around, people will hide them from you or come to you with every single question because they don't want to get in trouble. I like to hold them accountable but to minimize the mistake and focus on the learning from it. I talk about mistakes a lot in our company meeting but I never shame the person or call them out unless they want to. My best leaders will actually try to find how they can take responsibility and wear it on their shoulders much like in the book *Extreme Ownership* by Jacko Wilnik and Leif Babin.

Mistakes cost money.

They cost time.

They cost reputation.

But they also teach lessons that no book or consultant ever could.

Early on, I tried to avoid being wrong. I wanted clean decisions. I wanted certainty. I wanted hires, systems, and strategies to work the first time.

They didn't.

And the moment I accepted that being wrong was part of the job, I became a better boss.

Not reckless.

Not careless.

But willing to learn.

Why School Lied to Us

In school, failure is something to be avoided at all costs.

In business, failure is tuition.

Every meaningful leap I've made came after something didn't work:

- a hire that failed,
- a system that broke,
- a strategy that stalled,
- a belief that turned out to be wrong.

Looking back, it all makes sense. The dots connect. It's easy to pretend you knew all along.

But in the moment? You don't.

Leadership requires believing in decisions you can't fully see yet. Sometimes they work.

Sometimes they don't.

But the learning only comes if you're honest enough to admit when you were wrong.

The Danger of Pretending You're Right

The real failure isn't being wrong.

It's pretending you're not.

I've seen leaders double down on bad decisions because admitting they were wrong felt like weakness. They protect their ego instead of their people. And the company pays for it.

When you model learning instead of perfection, something powerful happens.

Your team gets braver.

Feedback improves.

Problems surface earlier.

Because people aren't afraid of being punished for being honest.

Being Wrong Doesn't Remove Authority—It Builds It

One of the biggest myths in leadership is that admitting mistakes undermines authority.

In reality, it strengthens it.

People don't expect perfection. They expect fairness. They expect growth. They expect honesty.

When they see you learn, they learn.

When they see you adjust, they adjust.

And when they see you own mistakes without defensiveness, trust grows.

THE LEADERSHIP PRINCIPLES

Being wrong is not the opposite of success.

It's the pathway to it.

A's and F's don't live on opposite ends in business. They live on the same side. Both mean you tried. Both mean you learned. Both mean you're moving.

The only real failure is standing still because you're afraid to be wrong.

THREE THINGS TO DO THIS WEEK

1. **Revisit one decision you were wrong about.** What did it teach you? What did it make better?

2. **Look for leadership potential where you didn't expect it.** You may be wrong in the best possible way.

3. **Model learning out loud.** Let your team see that growth beats ego every time.

LEADERSHIP
REQUIRES BELIEVING
IN DECISIONS YOU
CAN'T FULLY SEE YET.

— MARK STONER

CHAPTER 14

Vision Isn't a Poster — It's a Promise

Vision is easy when things are going well.

When revenue is climbing.

When trucks are being added.

When everyone can feel momentum.

You put numbers on a whiteboard. You talk about growth. You paint a future people want to be part of. And because the evidence is visible, belief comes naturally.

Vision gets much harder when things are declining.

That's when vision stops being inspirational and starts being a test of leadership.

When the Numbers Stop Working

Coming out of the COVID boom in 2022 and 2023, we hit a season I hadn't experienced in a long time.

Inflation was brutal. Costs were rising weekly. Materials, labor, insurance—everything was going up. At the same time, customers were pulling back. They weren't buying the way they had before. Our sales process wasn't working like it used to.

Revenue slowed. Margins tightened. Cash got uncomfortable.

For the first time in fifteen years, I was facing layoffs.

That alone was heavy. But what made it worse was *who* was feeling it.

Senior technicians were doing fine. Some were even complacent. Meanwhile, newer apprentices and overhead team members—the people with the least control over revenue—were the ones at risk.

That didn't sit right with me.

We needed to raise prices to survive. But raising prices created another problem. Our commission structure meant that while dollar amounts held, percentages *looked* lower.

From the technician's perspective, it felt like a pay cut.

I didn't like it.

They didn't like it.

But we were running out of cash.

This is where vision matters most.

Telling the Truth When You Don't Know the Ending

I called a meeting with senior leadership and key technicians.

I didn't sugarcoat it.

I told them exactly where we were. I explained the cash reality. I showed how inflation was eating margin. I told them we had already gone two years without raises or bonuses at the leadership level.

And then I said the part that made the room uncomfortable.

"I'm pissed that some of you are fine with this while other people are getting laid off."

That meeting wasn't well received.

That meeting definitely got my point across.

But something else happened too.

The people who stayed leaned in.

The company stabilized.

And we came out stronger.

Vision isn't about pretending everything will be okay. It's about being honest about where you are *and* clear about where you're going—even when you're not 100% sure how you'll get there.

The Hardest Part of Vision: Belief Without Proof

Looking back, it's easy to connect the dots and make leadership decisions look inevitable. In real time, they're anything but.

When you're in decline, vision requires hope without evidence.

You're asking people to believe in decisions they can't see working yet. You're asking them to stay committed while uncertainty is high and confidence is low.

That's not manipulation.

That's leadership.

And it's terrifying.

There were moments in that season where I didn't know if the decisions would work. I believed they *could* work. I believed they *needed* to be tried. But certainty? That didn't exist.

What I knew was this: if I wavered, the company would fracture.

Vision doesn't mean you're sure.

It means you're committed.

Structural Vision Is Still Vision

Most owners think vision is only about growth.

It's not.

Vision also shows up in:

- pay structure changes,
- process resets,
- organizational shifts,
- pulling back before you can move forward.

We had to fix things as we grew. Some systems that worked at three million didn't work at ten. Some pay structures needed adjustment. Some roles needed redefining.

Every one of those changes created anxiety.

Vision isn't just saying "we're growing."

It's saying, "Here's why this is changing, here's what it means for you, and here's what success looks like on the other side."

If you don't explain that, people assume the worst.

When Silence Kills Belief

I've watched companies die slowly because leadership went quiet.

Owners stop talking when things get hard. They retreat into spreadsheets and stress. They assume silence prevents panic.

It doesn't.

Silence creates fiction.

People make up stories about money, motives, and futures. And those stories are almost always worse than reality.

Even bad news, clearly explained, builds more trust than no news at all.

Vision Requires Follow-Through

Here's the part most people miss.

Vision without follow-through is worse than no vision at all.

If you tell people where you're going and then fail to act consistently with that direction, credibility collapses. Every promise becomes suspect. Every change feels manipulative.

Vision isn't what you say once.

It's what you reinforce over time.

You earn belief by doing what you said you would do— especially when it costs you something.

THE LEADERSHIP PRINCIPLE

The boss owns vision.

Not HR.

Not consultants.

Not posters on the wall.

The boss.

Your job is to tell people:

- where you're going,
- why you're going there,
- what it will require,
- and what it means for them.

And then to show up consistently until belief catches up.

Vision doesn't remove fear.

It gives fear direction.

THREE THINGS TO DO THIS WEEK

1. **Say out loud where the company is really headed.** Even if the path isn't clear yet.

2. **Explain one hard decision through the lens of vision.** Don't just announce it—frame it.

3. **Check your follow-through.** Vision lives or dies on consistency.

If You Don't Communicate, You're Letting Chaos Lead

"The single biggest problem in communication is the illusion that it has taken place." —George Bernard Shaw

Most problems in a blue-collar business don't start as big problems.

They start as silence.

Silence about expectations.

Silence about priorities.

Silence about what matters right now.

And when leadership goes quiet, something else always steps in to fill the gap.

Chaos.

Story One: Monday Mornings Were Killing Us

For years, Mondays were brutal.

Not because the work was hard—but because nobody knew what mattered most.

Technicians came in with different assumptions.

Office staff had unanswered questions.

Problems from the previous week rolled straight into the new one.

Everyone was busy.

Nobody was aligned.

I used to think meetings were a waste of time. I saw them as something white-collar companies did because they didn't have "real work."

That belief cost me years.

What I eventually realized was this: **we weren't short on effort—we were short on clarity.**

So we changed one thing.

We implemented short, structured morning meetings.

Not motivational speeches.

Not rambling updates.

Not gripe sessions.

Fifteen minutes. Standing up. Same agenda every time.

What we were seeing.

What mattered today.

What could hurt us if ignored.

And the chaos dropped almost immediately.

Same people.

Same jobs.

Different results.

Because clarity showed up before confusion could.

Communication Is a System, Not a Personality Trait

Early on, I relied too much on my personality.

I assumed people would "pick up" what mattered by watching me.

I assumed urgency would spread organically.

I assumed smart people would figure things out.

They didn't.

Not because they were dumb—but because **communication wasn't structured.**

The longer I ran the company, the more I realized this truth.

If something matters, it must be communicated repeatedly and deliberately.

Once is never enough.

Twice is rarely enough.

Ten times might be enough—if you're consistent.

Story Two: The Problem I Thought Everyone Knew About

There was an issue that kept popping up—small mistakes that created return trips and rework.

I was irritated.

I thought everyone knew it was a problem.

So I addressed it casually.

Once.

In passing.

It didn't change.

Then someone said something that stopped me cold:

"Mark, you mentioned it, but we didn't know it was *important*."

That stung.

I had confused **mentioning** with **communicating**.

Mentioning is casual.

Communicating is intentional.

From that moment on, if something mattered, it went into:

- the morning meeting,
- the written expectations,
- the training material,
- the follow-up conversations.

And suddenly, people weren't missing it anymore.

Short, Clear, Declarative Sentences Win

One of the best communication lessons I ever learned was this:

The more words you use, the less confident you sound.

All that did was invite debate.

Over time, I learned to communicate like a boss:

Short sentences.

Clear expectations.

No ambiguity.

This isn't harsh.

It's respectful.

People don't want speeches.

They want direction.

Story Three: When We Finally Got the Rhythm Right

Once we locked in consistent communication rhythms, everything changed.

Morning meetings set the tone.

Weekly leadership meetings solved problems before they spread.

Clear follow-ups eliminated guesswork.

People stopped asking the same questions.

Fewer mistakes happened.

Stress dropped.

Not because people cared more—but because **they knew what mattered.**

And here's the part most owners miss:

Meetings don't slow you down.

Unclear priorities do.

Meetings Aren't About Talking—They're About Alignment

Bad meetings waste time. Good meetings save it.

A good meeting answers three questions:

- What's happening?
- What matters right now?
- Who owns what?

Anything beyond that is optional. Meetings aren't for solving everything.

They're for preventing small problems from becoming big ones.

The Boss's Role In Communication

Here's the hard truth.

If your team is confused, it's not their fault.

It's yours.

The boss sets the communication standard.

That doesn't mean micromanaging.

It means **over-communicating what matters.**

Silence is never neutral.

It always favors confusion.

THE LEADERSHIP PRINCIPLES

You don't need better people. You need better communication systems.

And communication is leadership in motion.

THE VIDEO YOU SHOULD RECORD

Record a short video explaining:

- how communication works in your company,
- what meetings exist and why,
- what people should expect to hear repeatedly,
- how issues get surfaced and solved.

This becomes a cultural anchor.

THREE THINGS TO DO THIS WEEK

1. **Audit your communication gaps.** Where are people guessing?
2. **Standardize one meeting.** Same agenda. Every time.
3. **Say less—but say it more often.** Repetition builds confidence.

VISION DOESN'T REMOVE FEAR. IT GIVES FEAR DIRECTION.

— MARK STONER

Fair Isn't Equal — It's Clear

If you want to start a fight amongst your team, don't talk about politics.

Talk about pay.

Pay hits people in a place logic doesn't always reach. It taps into pride, fear, comparison, and stories people have been telling themselves long before they ever met you. That's why pay issues almost never sound like pay issues at first. They sound like morale problems, attitude problems, or "culture" problems.

Early in my career, I thought paying people well would solve most of that.

I was wrong.

Story One: When I Thought Generosity Would Fix Everything

When Ashbusters started gaining traction, my philosophy around pay was simple: be generous and people will reciprocate.

I paid above market.

I tried to take care of people.

I believed good pay would naturally lead to gratitude, loyalty, and ownership.

What I didn't understand then was this: **money doesn't fix confusion.**

It amplifies it.

If people don't understand how pay works, they don't see generosity — they see randomness. And when pay feels random, people fill in the gaps with stories. Those stories almost always end with the same conclusion:

"The owner must be getting rich on our backs."

That was almost never true. But I hadn't explained the truth either.

I didn't explain overhead.

I didn't explain margins.

I didn't explain reinvestment, risk, or retained earnings.

So silence did what silence always does — it let fiction take over.

The Quiet Resentment I Didn't See

In 2007, there was a season where the work was getting done, but something felt off.

Energy was low.

Complaints were higher.

Little comments started slipping out.

"You know how much this company makes. . . "

"Must be nice. . ."

"They don't see what we deal with. . ."

None of those statements were grounded in facts. They were grounded in assumptions.

That's when I realized something uncomfortable:

If you're not transparent, you're not neutral.

You're letting people invent a version of reality.

And they will.

Story Two: Why I Moved to Production-Based Pay

After trying hourly, salary, bonuses, and hybrids, I eventually moved most of our production technicians to production-based pay.

Let me be clear — **production pay is not perfect.**

It comes with real challenges:

- speed over quality,
- burnout if unmanaged,
- temptation to cut corners,
- short-term thinking.

But after everything I tried, I still believe it is the most *fair* pay structure in blue-collar work.

Not because it's equal.

Because it's clear.

When a technician is paid on production:

- doing it right the first time matters,
- callbacks hurt them too,
- efficiency benefits everyone,
- waste becomes visible.

It aligns the technician and the owner around the same outcome.

Not equal results — shared incentives.

That alignment changed everything.

Fair Isn't Everyone Making the Same

This is where people get tripped up.

Fair does not mean equal.

Fair means understandable.

Different roles create different value.

Different value creates different pay.

Different pay does not mean favoritism — it means function.

Once I stopped apologizing for that and started explaining it, tension dropped.

Not because everyone loved it.

Because everyone understood it.

Understanding builds trust even when outcomes aren't identical.

Transparency Changed the Conversation

When we became more open about:

- how jobs are priced,
- where money actually goes,

- what overhead really costs,
- why margins matter.

Something shifted.

The conversation moved from:

"Why do they get that?"

to

"How do I grow into more?"

That's a leadership win.

People don't need perfection.

They need honesty.

Story Three: When Pay Exposed a Standards Problem

I've seen production-based pay go sideways.

Technicians rushed.

Jobs got sloppy.

Customers were unhappy.

Rework ate margin.

At first glance, it looked like a pay problem.

It wasn't.

It was a standards problem.

Pay systems don't create behavior — they expose it.

Production pay without standards creates chaos.

Hourly pay without accountability creates drift.

Salary without clarity creates entitlement.

No pay structure fixes bad leadership.

The system only works when the boss works.

The Truth About Incentives

Owners often want a pay system that solves people problems.

There isn't one.

Pay systems only function when paired with:

- clear expectations
- inspection
- training
- consequences

In other words — bossing.

You don't abdicate leadership because a system exists. You reinforce it.

When It Goes Wrong (And It Will)

Every system needs guardrails.

When production pay started creating speed issues, we didn't scrap the system. We reinforced standards.

Clear workmanship expectations.

Clear consequences.

Clear accountability.

That's not being harsh.

That's being fair.

Because fairness protects the people doing it right.

The main ways we do this is to make the technicians redo the work without being compensated, removing part or all of the sales commission, making them go along with another technician to learn the correct way. I have learned that we best teacher is through their wallet.

Please check with local and state labor laws before taking any advice on pay structures.

A Boss Decision, Not a Popularity Contest

I've had people tell me directly they didn't like production-based pay.

That's okay.

A boss doesn't design systems to be liked.

A boss designs systems that work.

You listen.

You adjust when needed.

But you don't abandon structure because someone's uncomfortable.

Discomfort is often the price of alignment.

What Most Owners Miss

Owners avoid transparency because they think it will cause unrest.

The opposite is true.

Secrecy breeds resentment.

Transparency breeds respect.

Even when the numbers aren't great.

Even when the answer is "we can't afford that."

People don't need you to be rich.

They need you to be honest.

THE LEADERSHIP PRINCIPLE

Fair pay is not equal pay.

It's understandable pay.

When people know how money works, they stop making stories up.

When incentives align, effort aligns.

And when effort aligns, businesses scale.

THE VIDEO YOU SHOULD RECORD

Record a short video explaining:

- why you chose your pay structure
- what behaviors it rewards
- what it does not excuse
- how someone can earn more over time

This video kills rumors before they start.

THREE THINGS TO DO THIS WEEK

1. **Write down your pay philosophy.** If you can't explain it simply, it isn't clear enough.
2. **Identify where silence has allowed bad assumptions to grow.**
3. **Decide where transparency would calm things — even if it's uncomfortable.**

____

NO PAY STRUCTURE FIXES
BAD LEADERSHIP.

— MARK STONER

____

CHAPTER 17

Bring Water, Not Gasoline

Every company has stress.

The difference between a company that survives and one that implodes is not how much stress it faces — it's **how that stress is handled at the top.**

Leadership isn't about emotional absence.

It's about emotional *control* — and *intentional expression.*

The Weight of Emotion

Here's something most leadership books get wrong:

They tell you to control your emotions without ever explaining **why emotion matters.**

Emotion is information.

Not uncontrolled emotion.

Not explosive emotion.

But *measured*, intentional emotion.

When a leader who is usually calm shows concern, it carries weight.

When a leader who rarely raises their voice gets firm, people listen.

When you are emotional all the time, it loses meaning.

When you never are, it loses urgency.

The goal isn't emotional neutrality.

The goal is **emotional credibility**.

Story One: Almost Getting Stressed

I started wearing an Oura ring recently to track my sleep.

I've always been bad at sleeping enough. Too many years of early mornings, late nights, and thinking I could out-work fatigue.

The ring also tracks stress.

One day, my daughter Evane was showing me her stress readings. She had four to eight hours of stress registered in a typical day.

Then she asked to see mine.

Most days?

Zero minutes.

Occasionally?

Twenty to thirty minutes.

I took screenshots and sent them to her with a caption:

"Here's when I almost got stressed."

It was funny — but it was also revealing.

Stress doesn't disappear because you ignore it. It disappears because you **decide what deserves your energy**.

Leadership taught me this:

Most fires don't need gasoline. They need water.

Stress Is Contagious — So Is Calm

Teams mirror leadership.

If you panic, they panic.

If you react emotionally, they react emotionally.

If you create urgency without clarity, they create chaos.

But the opposite is also true.

When the boss stays composed under pressure, people feel safer.

When the boss absorbs stress instead of broadcasting it, people perform better.

This doesn't mean pretending everything is fine.

It means **being the shock absorber**.

Story Two: Watching A Leader Grow In Front of Me

One of the strangest parts of getting older in business is watching someone you love go through the same leadership lessons you already learned — and realizing you can't protect them from any of them.

I could see the problems coming.

I could see the mistakes forming.

I could see the outcomes before they happened.

And I still couldn't stop them.

Because leadership lessons don't transfer by warning.

They transfer by experience.

My daughter Evane has become a leader inside our chocolate company, Poppy & Peep as well as her own interior design business. She didn't grow into it the way I did. I came up through tools, trucks, and job sites. Her world is brand, people, product, and customer experience. Completely different environment — same leadership reality.

Early on, she cared deeply about everything working exactly right. When it didn't, she'd jump in emotionally and push hard to fix it. If something wasn't done the way she saw it, she'd bring a lot of energy to the situation.

Sometimes that energy helped.

Sometimes it poured gasoline on a small fire.

And without systems in place, her team loved her — but they couldn't always follow her. They wanted to make her happy, but they didn't always understand how to win.

I remember realizing she was going to have to learn the same lesson I learned years ago: people don't succeed because they care about you. They succeed because they understand what success looks like.

You can't just feel leadership. You have to define it.

She learned that the hard way. Not from me telling her. From situations not going the way she hoped they would.

Slowly, I watched her change.

- She started balancing emotion with accountability.
- She started understanding personality differences.
- She stopped trying to personally carry every outcome.

Instead of reacting, she began preparing.

Instead of fixing everything herself, she began guiding.

She learned to show love and compassion — but also clarity.

One thing she does better than I ever have is celebration. She celebrates her people constantly. Birthdays, milestones, accomplishments, family moments — she notices them and honors them. Her love language is definitely gift giving, and her team feels that. People want to do well partly because they know she actually sees them.

As I write this book, she's been honored by the Nashville Business Journal as a Woman of Influence. Watching that didn't make me proud because she succeeded.

It made me proud because she became a leader with a lot of my entrepreneur mindset and risk taking but finding her path in leadership.

She asks for advice — from me and from other business owners — but she filters it through her own instincts. And honestly, one of the places she seeks counsel most right now is ChatGPT.

That makes me laugh a little.

But it also makes a point.

Leadership isn't copying the previous generation.

It's learning principles and applying them in your own voice.

I learned leadership through pressure and correction.

She learned leadership through connection and awareness.

Different paths.

Same responsibility.

Your job as a leader isn't to create followers who act like you. It's to create leaders who don't need you.

When I started the business, everything depended on me.

Now I'm watching decisions get made, people get developed, and culture grow in ways I wouldn't have created myself — and that's how I know the company is healthier than it has ever been.

Because leadership didn't stop.

It multiplied.

THE LEADERSHIP PRINCIPLE

Your emotional state sets the emotional ceiling of
your company.

If you bring gasoline, expect fires.

If you bring water, expect stability.

Being calm doesn't mean being soft.

It means being strong enough to carry weight without
dropping it on others.

THE VIDEO YOU SHOULD RECORD

Record a video explaining:

- how you personally handle stress
- what deserves urgency in your company
- what does not
- how your team should interpret your reactions

This gives people a framework instead of guessing.

THREE THINGS TO DO THIS WEEK

1. **Audit where you're overreacting — and where
   you're underreacting.**

2. **Decide what truly deserves urgency.** Not
   everything does.

3. **Practice controlled emotion.** When you step out of
   calm, make sure it matters.

CALM IS ONLY
LEADERSHIP
WHEN IT'S PAIRED
WITH ACTION.

— MARK STONER

CHAPTER 18

Replace Yourself or Stay Trapped

Most owners say they want freedom.

Very few build toward it.

They talk about delegation.

They talk about working "on" the business instead of "in" it.

They talk about scale.

But then they quietly keep themselves at the center of every decision, every fire, and every approval.

That's not leadership.

That's job security disguised as control.

At some point, every boss has to face an uncomfortable truth:

If the business can't function without you, you don't own a business — **you own a very demanding job.**

Story One: When Growth Stopped Responding to Effort

For years, effort worked.

I worked harder, the business grew.

I stayed late, problems got solved.

I jumped in, things moved forward.

Then somewhere around the four to five million mark, effort stopped scaling.

I could work longer hours and still feel behind.

I could solve today's problems and wake up to ten more tomorrow.

That's when I realized something critical:

The bottleneck wasn't the market.

It wasn't the team.

It was me.

I was too involved.

Too central.

Too necessary.

The business didn't need more of my effort.

It needed less of my interference.

I had 17 employees and they all answered to me!

No real managers or hierarchy.

Every problem from "My pay check is wrong," to "Mrs. Smith is pissed," to "The parts are missing from the shipment," to "my van needs an oil change."

. . . was all me all the time.

Delegation Isn't About Trust — It's About Design

Most owners frame delegation as a trust issue.

"I just don't trust anyone to do it like I do."

"It's easier if I handle it myself."

"I'll delegate when I find the right person."

That's not a trust problem.

That's a system problem.

If your system only works when *you* are present, the system is broken.

Delegation is not about letting go.

It's about **building something that can hold weight without you.**

Story Two: Hiring Someone Who Did It Better Than Me

One of the hardest decisions I ever made was hiring a full-time Chief Operating Officer.

Up to that point, I had technicians making six figures on production-based pay — and I loved that. I loved seeing big checks go to people doing great work.

But this was different.

This was an overhead position.

Six figures.

No direct revenue attached.

And at the time, I was just starting to make a decent salary myself.

I was scared.

What I didn't understand yet was this:

If you hire the right person, they don't cost you money — **they make you money and give you time back.**

He and I could not have been more different.

I was the people guy.

He was the process guy.

And for a long time, that combination was magic.

We made the Inc. 5000 list three years in a row.

We were named a Tennessee Top Workplace six years in a row — an award voted on by employees, not executives.

That mattered to me.

Because it meant the business wasn't just growing — it was working.

Letting Someone Else Be Better Than You

Here's the part most owners won't admit:

Delegation threatens identity.

If someone else can do it better, faster, or more consistently than you, it forces a question:

"What am I actually here for?"

That question is uncomfortable — but necessary.

Your value as a boss is not in doing the work.

It's in **building the machine that does the work well.**

Story Three: Loving the Step Back

People assume stepping back is unsettling.

For me, it wasn't.

I loved it.

I loved growing leaders.

I loved watching others make decisions.

I loved taking longer vacations.

I loved having options.

For the first time, I could see the business running — not just surviving — without my constant presence.

That's when I knew we had crossed a line.

Not into laziness.

Into maturity.

Replacing Yourself Is a Discipline

Replacing yourself doesn't happen accidentally.

It requires:

- documented systems,
- clear authority,
- defined roles,
- trust built over time.

And it requires something else most owners resist:

The permission of imperfection.

Someone else doing it 80% right is almost always better than you doing it 100% right — because the 80% version scales.

The Trap of "I Love Doing the Work"

I hear this all the time.

"I just love being in the field."

"I enjoy the work."

"This is why I started the business."

That's fine — occasionally.

But every time you jump back into work that someone else should be doing, you're letting the team down somewhere else.

You are also taking away someones job.

Leadership work doesn't feel productive.

It doesn't create immediate wins.

It's invisible when done well.

But without it, nothing else works.

The Final Job of the Boss

At some point, the job of the boss changes.

Early on, it's about survival.

Then it's about growth.

Then it's about optimization.

Eventually, it becomes about continuity.

Can this business extend past me?

Can it thrive without my daily involvement?

Can it carry my standards forward?

That's the final test.

THE LEADERSHIP PRINCIPLE

If you want to be in charge of everything, you will be in charge of nothing that lasts.

A great boss replaces themselves on purpose.

Not because they don't care.

Because they care enough to build it right.

THE VIDEO YOU SHOULD RECORD

Record a video explaining:

- what decisions you no longer make,
- who owns what authority,
- how mistakes are handled,
- what success looks like without you.

This gives leaders permission to lead.

THREE THINGS TO DO THIS WEEK

1. **List what only you should do.** It's probably less than you think.

2. **Identify one role you're holding onto unnecessarily.**

3. **Begin replacing yourself — intentionally.**

CHAPTER 19

If You're Not Learning, You're Shrinking

One of the most dangerous lies a boss can believe is this:

"I've got this figured out."

The moment you think you've arrived is the moment decay begins. Not dramatically. Quietly. Slowly. Almost politely.

In blue-collar businesses, this shows up in subtle ways. You keep using the same systems that used to work. You rely on instincts that were sharp ten years ago. You stop seeking new inputs because you're busy "running the company."

That's not confidence.

That's stagnation.

Story One: When My Growth Outpaced My Skillset

There was a stretch in my career where the business grew faster than I did.

Revenue was climbing. Locations were expanding. Headcount was up.

On paper, it looked like success.

Internally, I was scrambling.

The problems were bigger than anything I had faced before. People problems. Systems problems. Decision fatigue. Issues that didn't have clear answers.

I couldn't outwork them anymore.

That's when I realized something humbling: **the version of me that built the company couldn't lead the company where it was going.**

I needed to learn.

Not casually.

Not occasionally.

Intentionally.

Learning Is a Leadership Responsibility

I started reading differently.

Not for entertainment.

Not for motivation.

But for tools.

Larry Winget once told me that if you will read 100 books on any subject, you will be a world class expert.

I didn't just read them.

I applied them.

I talked about them.

I tested ideas inside the business.

Reading wasn't personal development anymore.

It was operational.

Story Two: The Books That Changed How I Led

There are a handful of authors who fundamentally re-shaped how I think.

Larry Winget challenged my tolerance for excuses.

Scott McCain sharpened my understanding of differentiation and clarity.

Randy Pennington helped me think differently about change and adaptability.

These weren't "feel good" books. They were mirrors.

They forced me to ask better questions:

- Why do I tolerate this?
- What am I avoiding?
- What system is failing here?
- Where am I the bottleneck?

Learning like that is uncomfortable — but necessary.

Reading Isn't the Point — Application Is

Most people gather knowledge.

Very few execute.

Knowledge is not power.

Execution is.

You don't get credit for what you know.

You get results from what you apply.

Every book that mattered to me changed something about how we operated. A meeting structure. A hiring decision. A way of communicating expectations.

If it didn't change behavior, it didn't matter.

Story Three: Delegation Forced Me to Learn Faster

Delegation accelerates learning.

It made me feel like I had to stay ahead of everything to keep creating opportunities for my team and to not get beat in the marketplace

When you're no longer doing the work yourself, you're forced to think at a higher level. You can't rely on muscle memory. You have to rely on clarity.

Delegating forced me to:

- articulate expectations clearly,
- define success objectively,
- explain the "why" without rambling,
- build systems instead of heroics.

Every time something broke, it exposed a gap — not in the team, but in my leadership.

Those gaps became my curriculum.

Learning Keeps You Humble

One of the best side effects of continuous learning is humility.

When you're learning, you're reminded that:

- you don't know everything,
- others have solved problems you're facing,
- your way isn't the only way.

Ego kills learning.

And ego kills companies.

The best bosses I know are relentlessly curious. They ask questions. They listen. They seek perspectives that challenge their assumptions.

They don't confuse experience with infallibility.

What You Study Shapes What You Build

This matters more than most people realize.

If you only study your trade, your business becomes technical.

If you study leadership, your business becomes scalable.

If you study systems, your business becomes durable.

I've always believed this:

You become what you study.

That's why I chose to study business, leadership, and people — not just codes and techniques.

Learning Creates Optionality

Learning doesn't just make you better at today's problems.

It gives you options.

Options to pivot.

Options to delegate.

Options to step back.

Options to exit.

When you stop learning, options disappear.

The Boss's Learning Obligation

Here's the hard truth:

Your team cannot outgrow you.

If you stop learning, the business stalls — no matter how good your people are.

Leadership growth is not optional.

It's the job.

THE LEADERSHIP PRINCIPLE

The best bosses are students first.

They don't wait for crisis to learn.

They don't outsource thinking.

They don't rely on past wins.

They grow so the business can grow.

THE VIDEO YOU SHOULD RECORD

Record a short video sharing:

- what you're currently learning,
- why it matters to the company,
- how it's influencing decisions,
- what books or ideas shaped you.

This models growth as a cultural expectation.

THREE THINGS TO DO THIS WEEK

1. **Audit what you're currently learning.** Is it challenging you or just affirming you?
2. **Apply one idea immediately.** Knowledge unused is wasted.
3. **Make learning visible.** Talk about it with your team.

MOST PEOPLE GATHER
KNOWLEDGE. VERY FEW
EXECUTE. KNOWLEDGE IS
NOT POWER. EXECUTION IS.
YOU DON'T GET CREDIT FOR
WHAT YOU KNOW. YOU
GET RESULTS FROM WHAT
YOU APPLY.

— MARK STONER

Monthly Report

CHAPTER 20

You're Going to Be Wrong — That's Not Failure

If you're not wrong sometimes, you're not stretching.

If you're never surprised, you're not growing.

If everything is predictable, you're playing too small.

The only real failure in business is refusing to learn from being wrong.

Being Wrong Isn't Weakness — Staying Wrong Is

Here's the part that separates good bosses from fragile ones.

Fragile leaders hide from being wrong.

Strong leaders adjust.

If your ego is tied to always being right, you'll miss incredible people, cling to broken systems, and defend bad decisions far too long.

Being wrong is inevitable.

Staying wrong is a choice.

Leadership doesn't always announce itself.

Sometimes the people you least expect rise the highest—if you're humble enough to notice.

Again, I was wrong.

And again, that wasn't failure.

That was growth.

Business Isn't About Avoiding Mistakes

One of the most dangerous myths in entrepreneurship is that good leaders "just know."

They don't.

They test.

They adjust.

They fail forward.

Every company you admire is standing on a pile of mistakes that someone took responsibility for.

I've said this for years, half-joking but completely serious:

"To build a large company, you have to buy a lot of mistakes."

Mistakes cost money.

They cost time.

They cost pride.

But they also buy clarity.

When Being Wrong Hurt — But Mattered

As the company scaled, I had to come to grips with something uncomfortable.

Everyone's version of "right" was different from mine.

Quality.

Urgency.

Ownership.

I used to joke that at Ashbusters, "We get it right the third time."

That was sarcasm—but there was truth in it.

Scaling means you put your name on some work that isn't perfect. You buy mistakes while you build systems that prevent them next time.

The moment that really landed for me was realizing this:

If I jumped in to fix everything myself, we'd never grow.

Being wrong—letting things break, learning why, and fixing the system—was the only path forward.

That wasn't comfortable.

But it was necessary.

Why School Thinking Breaks Business Owners

School rewards certainty.

Business rewards adaptability.

In school, getting something wrong ends the conversation.

In business, getting something wrong **starts** the conversation.

What went wrong?

Why did it happen?

What system allowed it?

How do we prevent it next time?

If you treat mistakes as personal failures, your team will hide them.

If you treat mistakes as data, your team will surface them early.

That difference determines whether a business survives scale.

The Boss's Responsibility When Wrong

Being wrong doesn't absolve responsibility.

It increases it.

When a boss is wrong, the response matters more than the mistake.

Do you:

- defend the decision?
- shift blame?
- minimize the impact?

Or do you say:

"I missed this."

"That's on me."

"Here's what we're changing."

That moment builds trust faster than a hundred correct decisions.

Psychological Safety Comes From Ownership

People don't expect perfection.

They expect honesty.

When leaders own mistakes:

- teams speak up sooner,
- problems surface faster,
- learning accelerates.

When leaders pretend they're never wrong:

- silence grows,
- fear increases,
- reality gets distorted.

THE LEADERSHIP PRINCIPLE

You are going to be wrong.

About people.

About timing.

About systems.

About strategy.

That is not failure.

Failure is refusing to learn.

Failure is clinging to ego.

Failure is letting pride outrun progress.

Great bosses aren't right all the time.

They're **responsive all the time**.

THE VIDEO YOU SHOULD RECORD

Record a video sharing:

- a decision you got wrong
- what you learned from it
- what changed because of it
- how mistakes are handled in your company

This gives your team permission to learn instead of hide.

THREE THINGS TO DO THIS WEEK

1. Identify one place you might be wrong right now.

2. Be honest.

3. Ask someone you trust where you're missing something.

4. Decide how you'll respond when the next mistake shows up.

FRAGILE LEADERS
HIDE FROM
BEING WRONG. STRONG
LEADERS ADJUST.

— MARK STONER

CHAPTER 21

The Seat Feels Different Now

I didn't set out to become this version of a boss.

Early on, I was just trying to survive. Trying to make payroll. Trying not to screw things up too badly. Trying to prove — mostly to myself — that I could actually do this.

Back then, the boss's seat felt heavy in a very different way.

It was pressure without perspective. Responsibility without margin. Decisions made fast because there wasn't time to slow down.

I thought that feeling would go away once the company got bigger.

It didn't.

What Changed Wasn't the Pressure — It Was Me

What I've learned over time is that pressure never really leaves. It just changes shape.

Early pressure is financial.

Later pressure is people.

Then systems.

Then legacy.

The real shift didn't happen when revenue grew or when the company became "successful" by outside standards. It happened when I stopped needing to be everywhere.

The first time I took a long vacation and didn't panic...

The first time a major decision got made without me. . .

The first time a problem got solved before it reached my desk. . .

That's when I realized something had changed.

Not the business.

Me.

I Used to Think Control Was the Job

If I'm honest, I used to believe being a good boss meant being deeply involved.

Knowing everything.

Approving everything.

Fixing everything.

I told myself that was leadership.

What it really was, most of the time, was fear wearing a productivity costume.

Fear that if I stepped back, things would fall apart.

Fear that standards would slip.

Fear that people wouldn't care as much as I did.

Some of that fear was justified — early on, it *would* have fallen apart.

But I didn't always update my beliefs as the business grew.

Learning to Let Go Without Letting Standards Go

The hardest lesson wasn't delegation.

It was **trusting systems instead of instincts**.

Instincts got me here — but they couldn't take me where the business was going.

Letting go didn't mean becoming distant.

It meant becoming clearer.

Clearer expectations.

Clearer authority.

Clearer lines.

And once those were in place, I didn't have to hover anymore.

That was freeing in ways I didn't expect.

I Loved This Phase More Than I Thought I Would

People assume stepping back is unsettling.

For me, it wasn't.

I loved it.

I loved watching leaders grow.

I loved seeing people I hired make decisions I never would have made — and watching them work.

I loved the quiet confidence of knowing the business didn't need me in every room.

I loved the options.

More time.

More flexibility.

More perspective.

That's when I realized something important:

I wasn't losing relevance.

I was gaining range.

The Seat Looks Different From Here

I think back to that young technician who told me he wanted my seat.

At the time, I told him the truth: he couldn't see what came with it yet.

That wasn't arrogance.

It was experience.

Because the seat looks great from the outside.

From the inside, it's lonely at times.

Heavy at times.

Demanding even when things are going well.

But here's the part I didn't know how to articulate back then:

The seat gets lighter when you build the right people, systems, and culture around it.

Not easier.

Just lighter.

The Unexpected Calm

One of the most surprising things about this stage of my career is how calm it feels.

Not because nothing goes wrong — plenty still does.

But because I no longer feel personally responsible for *everything* going right.

Instead of saying "what do I need to do about it," I talk to the person in that division and say "what are you going to do about it."

When there needs to be something new done, I tap someone or hire someone to do the role.

When my daughter and I started our chocolate company, I learned how to make everything and for the first few months, I made everything but the entire time I knew that I was going to build this process and job for someone else.

I now do that with many, many new things. I learn it first, if possible, and then I hand it off to someone that will eventually be much better than me. I love that!

That's a subtle shift, but a profound one.

The company can handle stress now.

The leaders can handle decisions.

The systems can handle pressure.

That didn't happen by accident.

It happened because I stopped trying to be the solution and started building them.

I'm Not Done — I'm Just Done With This Chapter

I don't see this moment as an ending.

It's a transition.

I still love the work.

I still love building.

I still love helping people figure things out.

But I'm clear about where my energy belongs now.

Helping more owners avoid the mistakes I bought the hard way.

Helping them grow without burning out.

Helping them understand that being a boss isn't something to apologize for.

It's something to grow into.

What I Know Now That I Didn't Then

If I could sit down with my younger self — the version of me white-knuckling decisions and trying to hold everything together — I'd tell him this:

You don't have to carry it all forever.

You just have to carry it long enough to build something better.

The goal isn't control.

It's continuity.

The goal isn't being needed.

It's being replaceable.

The goal isn't proving how hard you work.

It's building something that works without proving anything at all.

Why I'm Comfortable Calling Myself a Boss Now

I used to flinch at the word.

Now, I don't.

Because I've learned what it actually means — not in theory, but in practice.

It means responsibility.

It means decision-making.

It means owning outcomes.

It means bringing calm when things are chaotic and clarity when things are unclear.

And it means knowing when it's time to step back — not because you're tired, but because you've done the job well.

The Seat Still Has Weight — Just a Different Kind

The seat still carries responsibility.

But now it also carries gratitude.

Gratitude for the people who stepped up.

Gratitude for the mistakes that taught me.

Gratitude for the seasons that stretched me.

And gratitude for the fact that I don't have to be everything anymore.

One Last Thought

If you're reading this and still in the thick of it — buried in decisions, pressure, and responsibility — know this:

It doesn't get easier.

But it does get clearer.

And clarity changes everything.

BUILD SOMETHING THAT FEEDS FAMILIES, GROWS PEOPLE, AND OUTLASTS YOU. THE WORLD DOESN'T NEED FEWER BOSSES. IT NEEDS BETTER ONES.
— MARK STONER

The Boss Manifesto

We were told bosses are outdated.

That leaders should be soft-spoken facilitators.

That authority should apologize for existing.

That idea has done real damage to blue-collar businesses.

Because blue-collar work does not need less authority.

It needs **better authority**.

A great boss is not a tyrant.

A great boss is not a friend.

A great boss is not afraid of being misunderstood.

A great boss brings **direction, clarity, and calm** into environments that are physical, dangerous, fast-moving, and unforgiving.

A great boss understands this truth:

People don't want less structure.

They want **fair structure**.

They don't want less accountability.

They want **clear accountability**.

They don't want chaos disguised as freedom.

They want **standards they can trust**.

A great boss sets the bar — **then protects it**.

They protect the team from bad behavior.

They protect the culture from erosion.

They protect the company from the slow leaks that quietly kill businesses.

A great boss does not hide behind consensus.

They listen.

They gather input.

They ask questions.

Then they decide.

Because indecision creates anxiety.

And anxiety spreads faster than clarity ever will.

A great boss understands that **respect beats likability every time**.

You don't need to be loved to run a company.

You need to be trusted.

And trust is built when people know where the line is —
and that it doesn't move based on mood, season, or who's
standing in front of you.

A great boss does not confuse kindness with avoidance.

They have the hard conversation early.

They correct in small doses.

They confront issues while they're still manageable.

Because what you tolerate becomes the standard — **every
single time**.

A great boss builds systems so people can win.

Training is not optional.

Clarity is not optional.

Measurement is not optional.

Not because people are bad — but because **good people fail
in bad systems**.

A great boss replaces themselves on purpose.

They delegate authority, not just tasks.

They build leaders, not dependents.

They create a business that works without their constant
presence — not because they don't care, but because they
care enough to build it right.

A great boss knows when it's time to step back.

Not out of burnout.

Not out of fear.

But out of maturity.

They understand that the final job of a boss is not control — **it's continuity**.

And when they finally exit, the business doesn't fall apart.

It runs smoother.

Calmer. Stronger.

That is not weakness.

That is mastery.

So call yourself a boss. Own it.

Be demanding and fair.

Clear and human.

Calm under pressure.

Direct without cruelty.

Build something that feeds families, grows people, and outlasts you.

The world doesn't need fewer bosses.

It needs **better ones**.

BE THE BOSS YOUR
BUSINESS NEEDS,
THE BOSS YOUR PEOPLE
CAN TRUST, AND THE BOSS
YOUR FUTURE SELF WILL
THANK YOU FOR
HAVING THE COURAGE
TO BECOME.

— MARK STONER

About the Author

Mark Stoner is a lifelong entrepreneur, tradesman, and business builder with nearly 40 years in the blue-collar world.

He is the founder of **Ashbusters Chimney Service**, one of the largest and most respected chimney and fireplace companies in the United States, along with multiple other operating companies across service, manufacturing, and training. Under his leadership, his businesses have grown to more than **$15 million in annual revenue**, been featured on **CNBC's *Blue-Collar Millionaires***, and earned recognition as a **Tennessee Top Workplace**—an award voted on by employees for ethics and culture.

Mark is also the co-founder of **SureFire Training Academy**, a national training platform built to professionalize and elevate the trades through structured apprenticeship, technical education, and leadership development.

His first book, *Blue-Collar Gold*, has sold **over 50,000 copies worldwide** and became a trusted resource for tradespeople and service-business owners looking to build companies from the ground up. He also hosts the long-running **Blue-Collar Gold Podcast**, where he shares unfiltered lessons from the field and conversations with business owners navigating growth, failure, and responsibility.

Today, Mark consults with hundreds of companies each year and is transitioning from day-to-day operations to focus on what he cares about most: helping blue-collar business owners build companies that are safer, stronger, and capable of outlasting them.

He lives in Tennessee with his wife, Terry, and is proud of the leaders his children are becoming—both in business and in life.

Enjoyed the Book?

If this book helped you, inspired you, or taught you something new, would you take a moment to leave a short review on the platform where you purchased it?

Reviews help other readers discover books they'll love—and they make a tremendous difference for independent authors.

Thank you for your support.